reality-centered learning

reality-centered learning

HY RUCHLIS

Adjunct Professor
in Education
Fairleigh Dickinson University

BELLE SHAREFKIN

Associate Professor
in Education
Brooklyn College
City University of New York

CITATION PRESS   NEW YORK   1975

FOR REPRINT PERMISSION, GRATEFUL ACKNOWLEDGMENT IS MADE TO:

E. P. Dutton & Co., Inc. for an excerpt from *Nigger: An Autobiography* by Dick Gregory with Robert Lipsyte, copyright © 1964 by Dick Gregory Enterprises, Inc.

Fort Myers News-Press for "Cold Unrelated to Colds."

The New York Times for "Marseilles and Arabs Are Uneasy" by Oliver G. Howard, © 1973 by The New York Times Company.

LIBRARY OF CONGRESS CATALOGING IN PUBLICATION DATA

Ruchlis, Hyman.
  Reality-Centered learning.

  Includes bibliographical references.
  1. Teaching. 2. Learning, Psychology of. 3. Educational innovations. I. Sharefkin, Belle, joint author. II. Title.
LB1025.2.R75   371.1'02   75-4849
ISBN 0-590-09602-8 (pap.)   ISBN 0-590-07433-4 (hdcr.)

PUBLISHED BY CITATION PRESS, LIBRARY AND TRADE DIVISION,

SCHOLASTIC MAGAZINES, INC.

EDITORIAL OFFICE: 50 WEST 44TH STREET, NEW YORK, N.Y. 10036

PRINTED IN THE U.S.A.

LIBRARY OF CONGRESS CATALOG CARD NUMBER: 75-4849

COVER DESIGN BY LUCY BITZER

75 76 77 78 79 5 4 3 2 1

ACKNOWLEDGEMENTS ♫

♫ "No man is an island unto himself," least of all the authors of this book. How does one acknowledge the myriad contributions of ideas from authors of books one has read, from ancient and modern philosophers of educational practice, from colleagues, and from students who have often provided insights? We therefore acknowledge indebtedness to many who must remain nameless.

We wish, however, to note the special contributions of those who offered assistance and advice. First and foremost, to Elsie Ruchlis who typed and retyped and re-retyped the manuscript, offering valuable suggestions for improvement as this essential task was done and redone.

Appreciation is also expressed to those who read the manuscript at various stages or who made special contributions to specific portions of the book: Phyllis Rubin, Dr. Lillie Pope, Dr.

Cecelia Pollack, Ruth Dropkin, Sylvia Newman, Jack Wengrow, Alice Wengrow, and Alan Stone, who assisted with the editing.

If we have omitted anyone whose name we have forgotten with the passage of time, our apologies for being human.

Hy Ruchlis
Belle Sharefkin

CONTENTS

INTRODUCTION ✆

✆ The American system of education is in a state of ferment and turmoil that reflects the profound changes taking place in our society. Pressures for changes in education stem mainly from the rapidly increasing complexity of a society that requires its citizens to confront constantly changing conditions and to become adept at solving a wide variety of new and difficult problems.

As John F. Kennedy commented, these problems arise from the fact that, "The world is very different now for man holds in his mortal hands the power to abolish all forms of human poverty and all forms of human life." The dilemma posed by these diametric alternatives is not likely to be resolved in mankind's favor without a new type of individual citizen who will not only adapt to change but help to make desirable change possible.

Edwin O. Reischauer has stated the problem in educational terms:

While the world is becoming a single great global community, it retains attitudes and habits more appropriate to a different technological age. . . . Before long, humanity will face many grave difficulties that can only be solved on a global scale. Education, however, as it is presently conducted in this country, is not moving rapidly enough in the right direction to produce the knowledge about the outside world and the attitudes toward other peoples that may be essential for human survival within a generation or two. This, I feel, is a much greater international problem than the military balance of power that absorbs so much of our attention today.[1]

In this grave situation it is not sufficient for education to depend solely upon the reliable old three Rs, although they are still necessary. Comprehension of social, political, and economic forces is now essential. Understanding scientific, mathematical, and artistic aspects of life is more important than before. Developing reasoning power, logical ability, and appreciation of individual and democratic values are urgent educational goals.

A school system that does not change in response to the powerful forces operating in our society, or responds too slowly, contributes to the feelings of frustration, irrelevance, and alienation observable in many students today. Its response must change not only educational content (what is taught) but, equally important, educational methodology (how it is taught).

The fundamental thesis of this book is that education can be more effective if its content is reality-centered—if what is taught focuses chiefly on what students feel is related to the real world around them. Methodology must also be reality-centered in the sense that teachers cannot assume some arbitrary state of mind or skill for students and impose upon them ways of learning that are not real and effective. Instruction and learning must be individualized and personally involve each student, not only with his mind

---

[1] *Toward the 21st Century: Education for a Changing World.* New York: Knopf, 1973.

but also his feelings and actions. *Methodology must be geared to the actual learner as he really is, not to some generalized, average abstract person.*

A curriculum maker should examine the total environment of students and determine those aspects of their lives that are significant to them or could be made so. Insofar as possible, teaching should be related to a student's reality, to what he or she feels is important. If the content of instruction helps explain the world to students and helps them to live in it, then they will be affected in positive ways and become eager to learn. If, in addition, teachers offer instruction in the form of personal, individualized experiences, with maximum involvement, integration of the senses, and at appropriate levels of abstraction, then learning is more likely to be effective and enjoyable.

These considerations do not mean that students are taught only what they want to know. Certain skills and knowledge are essential for maintaining civilization, and students must be taught such content and skills. By creating a reality-centered environment, the essential knowledge and skills are taught in a context that is as real as possible to students, thereby greatly motivating and strengthening their learning.

Reality-centered teaching does not neglect the abstract so essential to civilization. Abstractions can be very real for students, depending upon their stage of development, but the prevalent tendency to stress abstractions beyond the point where they cease to be real to students or can no longer be assimilated must be curbed. If that point is passed, the learner is put into an unreal environment, and education tends to become counterproductive.

Finally, exercising the imagination is an important part of life. Just think of how Isaac Newton's imagination helped shape our modern world. Imagination and creativity can be stimulated in the learning environment by designing real-life activities in the classroom and replacing some, but not all, of the current dominant unreal subjects.

The ultimate goal of such changes is to develop effective and affective learning environments, both in schools and outside, that will produce intelligent, active citizens who will continue to learn after their schooling because they learned how to learn and can adapt to the changing situations they encounter as adults.

It is one thing to set forth this goal—it is quite another to achieve it to a significant degree. Thus the problems of achieving the goals of reality-centered education are the main focus of this book. We will concentrate on the learner who is the recipient of the instructional process and the methods of instruction that illustrate how teachers can apply the principles of reality-centered learning.

THE NATURE OF
REALITY-CENTERED
EDUCATION

🍜 One of the authors of this book once lived in a twelfth floor apartment overlooking Prospect Park, a lovely oasis in the brick and concrete land mass known as Brooklyn in New York City. Looking out of the window over the tall trees in the Park toward the distant skyscrapers gave one a feeling of being removed from the hustle and bustle of city life. This unusual city scene is of special interest in explaining what is meant by reality-centered learning.

Focus your attention on the low hill in the middle distance. It is clearly much larger than the Park, stretching east and west as far as the eye can see. Actually the hill is part of a ridge that extends all along the northern edge of Long Island and is part of the terminal moraine that indicates the farthest advance of the glacier that covered the northern portion of North America some twenty thousand years ago. The ice slowly moved forward inch by inch, day after day, pushing rocks, trees, and debris from northern areas many miles away and finally dumping them helter-skelter where the ice melted each summer. So the ridge grew.

Below the hill is a lake, now quiet and peaceful, but ten or twenty thousand years ago it contained ice cold water from the melting snows, and in spring and summer the outflow was probably torrential.

When one stands on top of the hill in Prospect Park, it is possible, on a clear day, to see the rest of Brooklyn stretching out into the distance toward Coney Island and the ocean beyond. That flat expanse is the outwash plain formed by deposits of sand and mud washed out of the terminal moraine by the melting snows.

Are today's young people in Ocean Hill—located on part of the terminal moraine—ever made aware in their classes of the fascinating geological history of the land on which they live? The youth in the nearby communities of Crown Heights, Park Slope, Jackson Heights, Cobble Hill, Ridgewood, Forest Hills, Richmond Hill, Hillside, and Bay Ridge are probably equally ignorant. What potential lessons in those place names!

And the human history of this land! The Revolutionary War was fought all over the area. Do the kids on Lafayette Avenue, Kosciusko Street, Fort Hamilton Parkway, Franklin Avenue, Pitkin Avenue, Halsey Street, Hawthorne Street, Madison Street, Monroe Street, or Hancock Street know the history behind those familiar street names and the struggles of the men they honor? Teachers in schools near Fulton Street could relate the name to the invention of the steamboat. Lincoln Place and Union Turnpike could be the starting points of a study of the Civil War. St. Marks Avenue and St. James Place could initiate a study of the religion.

Then there is the geography inherent in street names: New Utrecht Avenue, Amsterdam Avenue, Albany Avenue, Schenectady Avenue, Rochester Avenue, and Pennsylvania Avenue. Wouldn't it be interesting for kids on Troy Avenue to correspond with live students in the city of Troy, New York, and describe their neighborhood and their lives?

And the mystery and potential poetry behind Gravesend Bay, Sheepshead Bay, Rockaway, Canarsie, and even of the name Brooklyn itself? Is Coney Island really an island? An old map would tell the story and reveal the dramatic changes that have occurred in the land.

When one examines the curriculum of the local school system, it becomes apparent that the real world "subject" of Prospect Park, so close to the lives of the people in the neighborhood, is essentially neglected. Elementary school classes may go on an occasional trip to the Park, perhaps to its zoo, but teachers are generally left to their own devices on how to relate the experience to the curriculum. Such trips are almost nonexistent at the secondary level, despite the wealth of applicability to real life. The reality-centered community resources of Prospect Park will not be used by the adjacent schools until the "subject" of Prospect Park is incorporated into the curriculum and the resource itself is developed with nature walks, museums, experienced guides, booklets, maps, and planned activities, fully supported by supervisors, planners, and the community. A similar disparity between the reality of the environment and the content of what young people are taught in school is evident in most communities.

Teachers may be experts in general, but not necessarily about specific local resources close to the lives of young people. Even if traditional subject-oriented teachers give a history lesson about the local area, do they think of considering its geology? If a teacher gives a natural history lesson, he or she would probably omit the human history. A physics teacher may not have any greater expertise in geology than a history major. These traditional subjects are not the realities of the students' world. Schools have an unreal subject-centered curriculum; they need a reality-centered curriculum.

Where are the reality-centered subjects of parents, friends, man, land and sea, materials, cars, airplanes, TV, homes, pollution, drugs, poverty, war and peace, inflation, or jobs? What youngster in the elementary grades would not enjoy learning about cars—

how the engine works, the purpose of the gearing system, driving safely, and the advantages of features of different cars. A large number of science and mathematics concepts are embodied in such learning and could readily be brought out. There is no dearth of content for abstract conceptual development in the reality of cars, but most curriculum makers are unaware of that potential because of subject area blinders. How many teachers know enough about cars to be able to teach youngsters about them?

There are reading specialists and math specialists and science specialists—why not car specialists? The study of cars is arbitrarily considered not an essential subject; this important reality is almost completely ignored. But it is not difficult to design a course about cars that touches upon many basic concepts and skills in science, mathematics, art, history, economics, and sociology and also requires reading and writing skills. It only seems difficult because most teachers have been trained in schools that stress abstract subjects. Actually, for young people, the progression from the reality-centered study of cars toward traditional abstract subjects is much more natural and fruitful than the reverse path taken today in schools.

Real subjects such as Prospect Park, man, cars, or airplanes are shunted aside because the traditional curricula begin with abstract concepts. But it should be the other way around—we should begin with the reality young people know and gradually move toward the abstract that they find difficult to comprehend.

THE GOALS OF EDUCATION

It is essential to view educational problems in the light of the following basic educational goals:

Imparting knowledge.
Developing a wide variety of skills, abilities, and mental processes.
Clarifying values and attitudes appropriate to society.

Developing the ability to integrate all of the above for intelligent decision-making and problem-solving.

In an earlier day traditional schooling stressed one of these—knowledge—in part because the other three goals were achieved to an acceptable degree at home and in the church and in part because the demands of the times were still relatively simple. Success in one's life's work usually did not depend upon mastery of the three Rs. The boy or girl who performed poorly at school might have been slightly handicapped in daily life, but there were no economic nor ego-shattering effects of the kinds a "poor" student suffers today. Furthermore, the school itself provided quiet, orderly instruction in a static environment that was not in basic conflict with other communications media and the outside world.

In contrast, today's interdependent civilization with its rapidly changing and increasing complexities imposes a heavy burden on education and makes its general goals more difficult to achieve with traditional methods and content. In the world outside school, students are continually bombarded by a variety of events, dramatically brought to their attention by television, radio, movies, and newspapers, all using complex symbols and abstractions. The static and obviously artificial environment of the school, proceeding along in its old ways, is at odds with the life styles students develop—a factor that greatly reduces the effectiveness of the school as an environment for learning.

In the process of planning activities to carry out the basic goals of education, it is helpful to take into account the wide variety of multi-levelled human behaviors that lead to learning. Systematic surveys of educational objectives by Bloom and others have spelled out human behavioral characteristics in what has come to be known as Bloom's taxonomy.[1] It defines three general areas

---

[1] Benjamin S. Bloom et al. *Taxonomy of Educational Objectives, the Classification of Educational Goals, Cognitive and Affective Domains.* New York: David McKay, 1956.

for educational goals: the cognitive domain (thinking and knowing), the affective domain (feelings, attitudes, and values), and the psychomotor domain (motion controlled by the mind).

The *cognitive domain* is further subdivided into the following increasingly complex levels:

1. KNOWLEDGE: Basic information, facts, and concepts.
2. COMPREHENSION: Awareness of the significance of information and its relationship to other information and ability to recall the information in a relevant manner when required.
3. APPLICATION: Using and applying knowledge and comprehension under different conditions. In a reality-centered curriculum, motivation for learning often begins with the application and then backtracks to fill in the required knowledge and comprehension.
4. ANALYSIS: Dissecting a problem into logical elements, seeing relationships, and distinguishing between facts, hypotheses, and principles.
5. SYNTHESIS: Putting knowledge into a new form, thereby creating a new piece of knowledge or creative behavior.
6. EVALUATION: Making judgments based on knowledge and evidence. This process involves the use of external criteria and value systems that affect the making of decisions. The evaluation area begins to impinge on the affective domain.

The *affective domain* is the area related to feelings, values, beliefs, and attitudes and relates to learning in fundamental ways. For example, a child brought up in a home where learning and reading books are contemptuously considered to be sissy stuff would most likely have little or no motivation to read and study. A student whose family is constantly in conflict with authority—police, courts, or schools—is not likely to enter a class favorably disposed to accept the authority of the teacher.

The following aspects of the affective domain are identified in approximate order of increasing complexity and priority:

1. RECEIVING: The learner must first be aware that information is being offered (he may be daydreaming), then he must be willing to receive it (he may be so angry he cannot listen), and finally he must offer controlled or selected attention (he may be unable to pay attention because of other factors such as hyperactivity, deafness, or poor vision).

2. RESPONDING: The learner is sufficiently motivated to respond to information. At the lowest level of intensity there is simple *acquiescence*, then, at a higher level, he is willing to respond, and at the highest level he obtains positive satisfaction in so doing.

3. VALUING: Specific behaviors are considered worthy and are favored or others are considered unworthy and are disfavored. At the lowest level of intensity a person merely accepts a specific value; at a higher level, he prefers it; and at the highest level, he is committed to it (perhaps by trying to convince others).

4. ORGANIZING A SYSTEM OF VALUES: Certain values are internalized and made an integral part of one's system of beliefs and attitudes.

5. ORGANIZING A COMPLEX OF VALUES OR A PHILOSOPHY: The various values are interrelated under a broad philosophy of life that determines what one chooses to learn or even to do.

The third area of learning, the *psychomotor domain,* is at present less well defined than the others, but it includes development of gross motor movements of the body, finely coordinated movements (hand-eye, hand-ear, hand-eye-foot, and so forth), non-verbal communication (gestures, body language), and speech behaviors (sound production, word soundings, spoken language).

The foregoing descriptions of the characteristics and levels of learning are, in effect, the learning realities schools should be dealing with. One is struck by the lack of relationship of this detailed list of mental functions to schooling as it is actually carried on today. Major stress is placed on just the first two aspects of the cognitive domain—knowledge and comprehension. Application occurs in an incidental way. Analysis, synthesis, and evaluation usually enter into the learning process in most subjects accidentally, if at all. Little or no attention is paid to the affective domain and its broad areas of values and philosophies. Even the receiving and responding aspects of learning are treated in routine, limited ways. Certainly the average gym class does not adequately treat the psychomotor domain, and this aspect of learning is considered, if at all, only when a student has a very obvious handicap, and often not even then.

A reality-centered approach will help schools develop the mental functions of students in many ways. It will:

Offer greater meaning to content, thereby improving motivation, attention, and response.

Provide more meaningful application to real situations.

Encourage analysis and synthesis by dealing with real problems.

Improve evaluation skills because there are more opportunities to evaluate when one deals with real things.

Include consideration of values because reality situations are inherently value-related.

Provide more opportunity for observing and correcting psychomotor deficiencies because students are called upon to do things.

IDEAL CHARACTERISTICS

There have been many attempts to describe the characteristics of an ideal process of education that can cope with today's demands. Terminology changes almost as rapidly as do fashions in dress. The current preferred terms are "individualized instruction," "individualized learning," "informal approach," "open classroom," or "environmental education." Yesterday it was "learning-by-doing," "project method," "core curriculum," "experience teaching," "discovery approach," "inquiry method," "investigating" or "activity program," "problem solving," "laboratory method," or "progressive education."

Naturally all these terms have somewhat different connotations depending on actual practice by proponents in the classroom. It is helpful to view them as descriptions of desirable characteristics of an ideal educational process that would feature individualized learning, informal settings, new experiences, performing investigations, doing projects, solving real problems, and working in labs— all leading to learning-by-doing.

Individualized learning is one of the major characteristics of the kind of education we advocate. All individuals differ, and the same thirty-to-one classroom instruction may or may not reach all students, or even most. Individualized learning solves this problem by dealing directly with the student, usually in one-to-one or small group situations. But it is also possible to reach students individually—at least some of the time—in standard thirty-to-one classroom situations. The point is that whatever the learning situation, the *individual* must be affected in a positive way by the instruction and learn concepts or skills that the teacher feels are necessary.

Learning-by-doing also expresses an important feature of the instructional process. The phrase is not limited to the narrow sense of physical doing with one's hands. A musician learns best by playing his instrument. A scientist learns best by "sciencing." A businessman learns by conducting a business. A teacher learns by teaching. A child learning to read should do so in the context of reading. Whatever one wants to do, he or she learns by doing it.

To say this is not to denigrate the value of formal instruction at appropriate times and in proper proportions. Facts and principles still have to be learned, and this is often effectively accomplished in traditional classroom situations. Learning-by-doing not only tends to enlarge the reality content of instruction but also offers opportunities for teachers to observe students in an individual setting and to help them learn.

MEANING OF REALITY

A person's notion of reality depends upon how his sensory impressions have been filtered through the screen of his mind, which consists of a multitude of concepts based on previous personal experience and cultural heritage. Obviously the real world is different to people of even similar age, background, and status and is substantially different for persons of widely different circumstances. Reality for the ghetto youngster who is black, Chicano, or Puerto Rican is very different from the reality of the college-bound, middle-class kid who grew up in suburbia.

In educational terms a reality-centered approach must take into account the widely different circumstances of the many worlds in which students live. It implies that educational content and methodology be individualized to meet the different needs of different types of students.

It should not be assumed that a reality approach adheres only to the mundane, materialistic, three-dimensional aspects of life. Anyone who has ever received a summons for speeding from a policeman who merely wrote a few abstract symbols on a piece of paper knows how real abstractions can be. Reality for a mathematician, a painter, a composer, an economist, or a poet is composed of many abstractions. This is also true at the lower levels of learning. What could be more abstract than the letter *a* or the number 2 printed on a page? Yet what could be more real in an educational sense?

There is no contradiction between a reality approach in education and teaching abstractions at any level. What the educational concept of reality does is to insist that whatever is taught be taken up in a context that is real to the student and thus is meaningful. The purpose of using the term reality is to focus attention on what teachers must do to make education meaningful to each student.

EDUCATIONAL ✿
REALITIES ✿

✿ The recent flood of books and articles criticizing and attacking educational methods—and even questioning the necessity of having schools at all—has been disconcerting to the hapless teacher who is trying to do his or her best in a difficult daily situation. Although the immediate effect often seems unsettling and destructive, the reexamination prompted by these criticisms is likely to change educational methodology for the better in the long run. Such an outcome will depend on how meaningful research and thoughtful criticism are used to effect learning in an educational system.

Basically, learning is a process in which an individual's conceptual state is altered both cognitively and affectively by interaction with the environment. The function of schools is to provide a learning environment that promotes conceptual development compatible with the goals and changes desired by society. But today we don't all agree on what these goals and changes should be or which ones have greater priority, nor does it follow that the learning interactions sought actually occur. School obviously fails for a destructive dropout who embarks on a life of crime. It seems to succeed for the "square" kid who minds his ps and qs and ends up with a job as a computer programmer with a wife and two kids in a suburban town—although there are some who would raise questions about the degree of success. The problem is complex because of varying goals and also because there are so many different aspects to the educational process, encompassing emotional, intellectual, physical, and psychological developments for widely differing individuals.

STAGES OF DEVELOPMENT

If the educational process is to be intelligently directed, it is essential that educators understand the general principles of the development of young people, the nature of the similarities and differences of students, and the characteristics of their interactions with other individuals, teachers, groups, and society. It is important that the learning process achieves the fundamental goals of education by attending to the needs of both the individual and society.

Current attempts to change patterns of school organization to meet widespread criticisms reflect the need to get away from the rigidities of mass education in which students are lockstepped into hard and fast curricula and required to march to its commands. With the exception of the almost defunct one-room school, most public schools today attempt to handle the learning levels of students by segregating them into classes based on age. The basic justification for age segregation is the fact that mental and physical developments proceed through distinct stages of increasing ability with increasing age.

Jean Piaget's description of the stages of development with approximate ages are outlined in the tables on pages 18–19. These stages provide educators general guides for instruction for specific age groups.

Although Piaget's concepts have not been widely applied in secondary classroom situations, it is probable that his ideas will eventually be incorporated into diagnostic procedures that can predict whether or not a given student is mentally ready for a given set of concepts. We could then avoid putting students into situations and courses for which they are not prepared.

Basically students can function effectively if an educational activity meshes with or enlarges previously acquired concepts. When students are confronted with a new challenge, they are forced to respond in a way that modifies old concepts or beliefs or develops new ones that incorporate (or sometimes reject) former concepts. Individuals integrate new concepts with former ones in ever increasing stages of complexity.

Each of these major stages is further separated into substages. For most students such changes occur in a framework of concrete and sensory activity, especially at the younger ages, but as they grow older, a larger proportion of changes are of an abstract nature.[1] This point is explored more fully in chapter 8.

Life for teachers would be greatly simplified if development proceeded on a completely uniform, predictable basis, with all young people reaching the same stage of mental development and comprehension at the same time and in most respects. But, as with all human characteristics, there is great variation, and classes determined by age alone contain a wide range of abilities, especially at older age levels, making it difficult, if not impossible, for the teacher to reach all students with the same instructional content or methods.

Variations in concept development may be much greater than are generally assumed. For example, in an investigation of students in grades seven to twelve in Oklahoma, tasks involving the

---

[1] Richard M. Gorman. *Discovering Piaget: A Guide to Teachers,* chapt. 4. Columbus: Charles E. Merrill, 1972.

PIAGET'S INTELLECTUAL

DEVELOPMENTAL STAGE	GENERAL AGE RANGE	CHARACTERISTICS OF STAGE PERTAINING TO PROBLEM-SOLVING ACTIVITIES, COMMENTS AND EXAMPLES
Sensorimotor	Birth to approximately 18 months	Stage is preverbal. An object "exists" only when in the perceptual field of the child. Hidden objects are located through random physical searching. Practical basic knowledge is developed which forms the substructure of later representational knowledge.
Preoperational or "representational"	18 months to 7–8 years	Stage marks the beginning of organized language and symbolic function, and, as a result, thought and representation develop. The child is perceptually oriented, does not use logical thinking, and therefore cannot reason by implication. The child is simple-goal directed; activity includes crude trial-and-error corrections. The child lacks the ability to coordinate variables, has difficulty in realizing that an object has several properties, and is commonly satisfied with multiple and contradictory formulations. Since the concepts of conservation are not yet developed, the child lacks operational reversibility in thought and action.
Concrete operations	7–8 years to 11–12 years	Thinking is concrete rather than abstract, but the child can now perform elementary logical operations and make elementary groupings of classes and relations (e.g., serial ordering).

[2] Anderson, DeVito, Dyrli, Kellogg, Kochendorfer, and Weigand. *Developing Children's Thinking Through Science* © 1970. Reprinted by permission of Prentice-Hall, Inc., Englewood Cliffs, N.J.

DEVELOPMENT STAGES[2]

DEVELOPMENTAL STAGE	GENERAL AGE RANGE	CHARACTERISTICS OF STAGE PERTAINING TO PROBLEM-SOLVING ACTIVITIES, COMMENTS AND EXAMPLES
Concrete operations	7–8 years to 11–12 years	The concepts of conservation develop (first of number, then of substance, of length, of area, of weight, and finally of volume in the next developmental stage).
		The concept of reversibility develops.
		The child is unable to isolate variables, and proceeds from step to step in thinking without relating each link to all others.
Propositional or "formal operations"	11–12 years to 14–15 years	This stage of formal (abstract) thought is marked by the appearance of hypothetical-deductive reasoning based upon the logic of all possible combinations; the development of a combinatorial system and unification of operations into a structured whole.
		The development of the ability to perform controlled experimentation, setting all factors "equal" but one variable (in substage IIIA the child's formal logic is superior to his experimental capacity). Individuals discover that a particular factor can be eliminated to analyze its role, or the roles of associated factors. Reversal of direction between reality and possibility (variables are hypothesized before experimentation). Individuals discover that factors can be separated by neutralization as well as by exclusion.
	14–15 years and onward	The individual can use interpropositional operations, combining propositions by conjunction, disjunction, negation, and implication (all arise in the course of experimental manipulations).

concepts of conservation of weight, solid amount and volume, elimination of contradictions, and exclusion of variables were presented. Only about one-third of the high school seniors in this study were above the concrete operational stage for the specific concepts Piaget had indicated as generally achieved at approximately age eleven for the children he studied.[3]

Another study involved 131 freshmen at the University of Oklahoma who were given similar tasks. Only half were operating completely at the concrete operational level for the specific concepts and skills investigated, a level Piaget states is generally completed by age twelve.[4]

This low achievement level of high school seniors and college freshmen does not necessarily mean that they were unintelligent. It may simply be that they had little or no experience with such specific phenomena as conservation of weight and volume and separation of variables. No doubt some experiences in the subject would bring most of these students up to par. All adults have similar weak spots in their mental constructs due to lack of experience with specific facts or ideas.

MATURATION OF STUDENTS

Teacher misjudgments of the potentials of students are quite common, often because they do not understand the process of maturation in education. They tend to predict the future by extrapolating from the present and past. For example, suppose that a top student, A in Figure 1, is progressing at a very rapid rate, indicated by a steeply rising line A'. Most people would assume continuation of this rate of progress and foresee a brilliant future, but the student's progress may be of the common flash-in-the-

[3] John Renner and William Ragan. *Teaching Science in the Elementary School.* New York: Harper & Row, 1968.
[4] J. W. Mackinnon and John Renner. "Are Colleges Concerned with Intellectual Development?" *Journal of American Physics,* vol. 39, September 1971, pp. 1047–52.

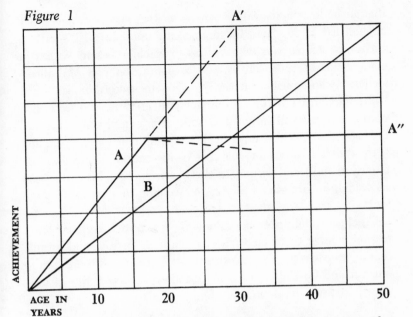

Figure 1

pan variety. Something may happen to his desire to learn, or he may experience a period of bad luck such as a personal tragedy or injury, or he may suddenly lose his ability to work, and his learning achievement may level off at a plateau, A".

On the other hand, a slower or average student, B, who progresses at a lower rate than A in his or her early years, may simply be maturing more slowly, or be mastering knowledge more thoroughly, or have more creative qualities, or be blessed with bulldog persistence. The lower rate of progress may continue without interruption. In the long run thoroughness, depth, steadiness, and persistence often pay off, and B may reach a higher level of learning achievement than A.

Similar considerations apply to social development. Students with considerable intellectual potential may fritter away their talents (or may seem to) in useless pursuits, but frequently such students "put it all together" when they decide what they want to do in life. No one is able to predict with any degree of certainty that an underachiever will remain so, or that an overachiever may not fall flat on his face. There are many examples of B's pattern and of underachievers who become overachievers and leaders in many fields of endeavor, as well as many examples of brilliant students who somehow never managed to succeed in later life. Consider Canada's Prime Minister Pierre Trudeau who seemed to wander aimlessly all around the world after completing his education and only buckled down to business at age twenty-seven and then went on to become a leader of his nation. What were his family, friends, and former teachers saying about his chances of succeeding in life after five years of seeming to accomplish nothing?

Teachers should not allow students' current achievement levels to shortchange them on time or attention. They should assume that all students have unknown potential which it is their duty to uncover and develop. They may not always succeed, but at least they should not stop trying.

FAILURE AND POOR SELF-IMAGE

It is often useless or destructive to assume a person is ready for a specific learning task if the prior groundwork is missing, no matter what the age or formally designed educational level. If experience is withheld too long, it may be difficult to provide compensatory experiences to build mental structures needed for specific concept development. It is not likely that a person deprived of experiences with mechanical devices during youth could become an outstanding mechanic as an adult, or that one could become a successful mathematician without competent training in appropriate concepts at an early age.

In the traditional thirty-to-one heterogeneous classroom, it is almost inevitable that some students will seem less able to master the required work. If a student finds himself at the bottom rung of the ladder in all subjects and in all classes, it does not take long to destroy his sense of worth and push him into a state where his behavior increasingly contributes to fulfilling everyone's expectations that he will not amount to much.

There is significant evidence that the expectations of teachers are reflected in the self-image of students and play an important role in success at school. In an experiment conducted by Robert Rosenthal and Lenore Jacobson, teachers were erroneously informed that tests revealed certain children in their classes to have special abilities and that they could be expected to do better schoolwork. It was found that these children then tended to fulfill expectations. Apparently, expecting better work from children altered the relationship between students and teacher to produce improvement.[5]

Some authorities have questioned aspects of this experiment. Nevertheless, the major point concerning the influence of self-concept, teacher attitudes, and classroom climate on learning is rooted in psychological and educational evidence.[6]

There is also evidence that even a student's name may be a factor in failure. What biases were operating when experienced teachers, marking essays of students they did not know, gave significantly lower ratings to those with unusual names like Elmer, Oswald, and Maude than to children with everyday names like David, Michael, Susan, and Sally? Interestingly enough, teacher trainees did not reveal such a bias. It can be hypothesized that students with unusual names are likely to be taunted by their classmates and react by becoming belligerent, aggressive, and antagonistic toward others, including teachers, who then counteract by anticipating difficulties before they occur. One investigator links female students' personality and behavior patterns to specific names. According to his research an Elizabeth tends to be likeable and intelligent, a Doris is gossipy and rather dull, and a Susan is

---

[5] *Pygmalion in the Classroom.* New York: Holt, Rinehart & Winston, 1968.
[6] Carl R. Rogers. *Freedom to Learn: A View of What Education Might Become.* Columbus: Charles E. Merrill, 1969; Gary Anderson. *An Assessment of Learning Environments.* Halifax, Nova Scotia: Atlantic Institute of Education, 1971.

just about average. A Harvard study found that young people with unusual names are more likely to fail than those with ordinary names.[7]

Whatever the cause, curable or not, inherent or environmental, escape from failure-producing situations at school is impossible for many girls and boys for the entire critical period of childhood and youth. Such situations are especially severe in neighborhoods that have overworked, discouraged teachers in dingy schools, a high degree of unemployment and poverty, poor housing, inadequate health care, and a high incidence of crime and drugs. Absence of books, newspapers, and intellectual discussion at home and lack of attention by harassed parents to basic preschool activities make it difficult for young people to adjust to the markedly different environment of school.

Even students from nondisadvantaged home environments may suffer a sense of failure, not because of their own inadequacies but because their learning styles do not conform to that required by the school. Some work at a slow but thorough pace and are often crowded out of the limelight by those whose classroom performance is quick-on-the-draw but superficial. The learning style of a student may also conflict with the teaching style of a teacher, who may misinterpret such a conflict as the student's inability to learn or even as willful stubbornness.[8] Many supposedly slow students blossom when learning shifts from the traditional sit-and-listen-to-the-teacher approach to learning-by-doing. Then initiative and imagination may become apparent in students who seemed to lack these qualities in the customary classroom setting.

The main task of education for "poor" or "slow" students is to break the chain of self-fulfilling prophecy by proving to them

---

[7] James J. Thompson. *Beyond Words: Nonverbal Communication in the Classroom.* New York: Citation Press, 1973.

[8] L. Heil et al. *Characteristics of Teacher Behavior and Competency Related to the Achievement of Different Kinds of Children in Several Elementary Grades.* Washington, D.C.: U.S. Office of Education, 1960; Wayne C. Frederick and Herbert Klausmeier. "Cognitive Styles: A Description," *Educational Leadership,* April 1970, pp. 668–72.

through personal, real experiences that they are capable of intellectual and creative accomplishment, that they can competently plan and carry out long-range tasks that have meaningful outcomes, and, finally, that they can experience a strong sense of enjoyment in doing so. New motivational approaches are required in which learning begins with reality-centered activities that bear little outward resemblance to traditional school programs. Of course, reading, writing, math, and other skills must be included.

Naturally, teachers can play a key role in altering a student's negative self-image. The late Haim Ginott, author of a popular series of books, provides some insights for teachers:

> Parents [and presumably teachers] ask why children are not our friends after all we do for them. The answer is: They are dependent on us, and dependency breeds hostility. It follows, then, that by diminishing dependency we can make friends of our children.
>
> The rest of the world is so eager to point out to children their wrongness; it is up to parents and teachers to use every opportunity for making children aware of their rightness. . . .
>
> *Give children choices. Offer them options.* I remember talking with a group of teachers who were also parents, and one said, "You're telling me to give choices to my pupils. I can't even do that with my own children."
>
> I asked, "How old is your youngest?" She replied, "Two years."
>
> I said, "Can you say to him, 'Danny, would you like to have your eggs hard or *very* hard?'" She answered, "Well, I think I could manage that."
>
> Then I asked her, "What difference does it make to Danny if you give him this kind of choice?" She concluded that Danny may say to himself, "My mother takes my wishes into account. I have something to say about my life. I am a person."[9]

9 "Driving Children Sane," *Today's Education*, November 1973, pp. 20–25.

That is the secret for building positive self-image at *all* ages. Everyone—child, student, parent, teacher—must be made to feel that, "I am a person." Any action or remark by a teacher that demeans a student or makes him feel less capable or less worthy or stupid—in other words, less of a person—tends to induce a negative self-image with lower self-expectation, less motivation, and reduced achievement. Any pleasant, friendly remark or action or encouragement by a teacher tends to build a healthy ego and a constructive, motivated person.

Finally, note that although it is essential to plan the curriculum to ensure successful learning, it is equally necessary to build in some *minor* degree of failure. A whole person needs to succeed in some respects and to fail slightly in others. Children who never experience failure, which they must struggle to overcome, may grow up into fragile adults who fall apart at the first inevitable failure in life.

It is a rewarding experience to succeed after a modest period of failure and struggle. Situations that encourage this type of experience should be built into the curriculum because of their importance to future achievement. This implies, of course, skilled, sensitive observation, particularly during the formative years, so that learning can be matched to individual needs for success and failure.

THE EDUCATIONAL DILEMMA

Although one teacher generally offers instruction to a class of about thirty, the effect of her or his efforts is eventually individual. One student grasps concepts readily, while another finds the same ideas difficult to comprehend; for still another the unintended effect may actually be destructive. Regardless of the method of instruction, what counts is the degree of individual learning.

The term "individualized instruction" is commonly used to indicate a setting in which a tutor or teacher gives instruction to small groups or even on a one-to-one basis. In many situations such a procedure is highly desirable and often essential, although it is much more costly when highly paid instructors do the teaching—an important consideration.

But generally teachers instruct a class of thirty students and attempt to involve each of them in learning what they have to offer. Perhaps Johnny is all ears, because he wants to once again excel on that next test or is eager to show how smart he is by popping up his hand to answer every question. But Sadie's mind is wandering because her father is ill and out of work. Fred, bored with all school business, is dreaming of hitting a home run during next Saturday's baseball game, with the crowd wildly cheering. Bess is fidgeting and wants to get up and move around, perhaps because she is hyperkinetic. Paul, who responds slowly, is filled with fear that if called upon he may stutter and his fellow students will laugh. Marcia dislikes the teacher because she is too strict and doesn't let her talk to her neighbors, so she gets even by not paying attention.

The content of a course teachers are required to teach and the varying states of mind of students and their different degrees of conceptual and emotional development tend to obstruct learning in a mass situation, producing a dilemma. In the traditional thirty-to-one class teachers usually cannot readily teach to reach all. If they teach to reach some, then others are inevitably neglected. Which group they neglect is often a matter of a Hobson's choice.

The pros and cons, the goods and evils of homogeneous versus heterogeneous classes cannot be completely resolved by traditional systems of classroom organization. If classes and schools are set up mainly for those who achieve academic excellence, then students are inevitably segregated by culture, background, parental income, and color. When that happens, society automatically reduces the equality of opportunity.

LEARNING-BY-DOING

Learning-by-doing activities can advance the psychological development of students by removing the lockstep pressure on them to perform exactly the same activities equally well. Each student can perform the activities on his or her own, and the destructive effects of constant comparisons with others, characteristic of the standard classroom, will be minimized.

In an individualized situation students should be given greater responsibility for their learning. They should be encouraged to exercise initiative in obtaining information, mastering procedures, and carrying out activities. They may need some help, but this is not generally a problem if an activity is appropriately designed and includes a variety of options. Frequently other students in the class or those from a higher grade can give assistance. When there is a framework of student responsibility for learning, the classroom atmosphere becomes more informal and less tension-producing, with fewer behavior problems.

Much depends upon the nature of the activities. If they have strong motivational content, they will stimulate even reluctant students to perform them, particularly if they are concrete rather than abstract and manipulative rather than word-oriented. Once fearful students have crossed the initial barrier, it will be quite natural for them to try similar activities that are the basis for conceptual development.

The general momentum of learning-by-doing activities by the majority often impels more reluctant students to participate. Sometimes such students become leaders in learning-by-doing because they excel in manipulative skills or in initiative or creativity.

An experiment relating to this phenomenon, performed by Arnold Miller for a master's thesis (New York University, 1960), is of interest. Teachers from three different classes—one fourth grade, one fifth grade, and one sixth grade—were asked to select their three best and their three poorest students in mathematics. All eighteen students were gathered in one room and given materials and instruction booklets for making polyhedral shapes (solid shapes with flat faces) using panels that could be connected together along the edges with rubber bands.

No observable difference between the best and poorest mathematics students was found in their ability to follow instructions and assemble the desired mathematical shapes. As expected, sharp differences were observed in the handling of abstractions concerning the recognition and naming of shapes.

At the conclusion of the activity, which lasted for a number of sessions, the experimeter asked the students to state some uses for knowledge about polyhedral shapes. After examining the responses, it seemed evident that some of the poorer mathematics students possessed insights into possible uses that were more creative than those listed by the better mathematics students. The responses were then duplicated in random order on sheets of paper and given to twenty teachers with the request that they subjectively rate the responses for indications of creativity. When the data were compiled and averaged, it turned out that the average rating for creative responses by the poor mathematics students was significantly higher than for the responses of the better mathematics students! Despite the obvious scientific weaknesses of the crude rating system, it is interesting that students rated very poor in mathematics seemed to do better than their classmates in some aspects of intellectual activity—in this case imagining uses for shapes they had just worked with.

These observations provided the basis for a simple experiment that has been tried with several groups of mathematics teachers. A polyhedral shape known as a cuboctahedron was displayed; it looks like a cube with its corners cut off. The mathematics teachers were asked to describe the properties of the shape by means of direct observation. Generally they performed at a surprisingly low level; few, and sometimes none, could see the essentially cubical origin of the shape. Few, or none, knew its name or had ever seen it before. These mathematics teachers were "disadvantaged" with respect to this type of mathematical skill of visualizing polyhedral shapes in three dimensions. This deficiency may be explained by the required mathematics courses at the high school and college level that tend to favor algebraic abstractions and ignore the study of real-life solid shapes, despite their importance in architecture, crystallography, and other fields of knowledge.

Could it be that poor students in traditionally abstract mathematics might do well in architecture, which involves a different set of abilities? Should the schools put many students in the position of failing certain subjects that they must take, while not offering others at which they might excel? A variety of learning-by-doing activities, even in a traditionally abstract area such as mathematics, is likely to reveal skills supposedly poor students may have and could give them a chance to excel—a vital factor in building feelings of self-worth.

Activity in and of itself does not solve all educational problems —it must be put into a context that is educationally productive for the individual. If a student has a long history of failure and is easily discouraged, more individual assistance should be given. It is important for the teacher to offer frequent encouragement and praise to foster increased self-confidence. Defeated students are unaccustomed to taking responsibility for their learning and require basic training in new approaches until they have built up sufficient self-confidence to be able to function on their own.

MATCHING LEARNING LEVEL
TO THE LEARNER

In the light of these considerations, the supervisor or teacher should consider whether a specific learning activity, course, or curriculum is planned at a pace students can successfully manage. If the pace is too rapid, students will become discouraged and defeated. On the other hand, if the general educational fare is too easy and repetitive or uninteresting and boring, students tend to dislike school because they are not learning and the school environment may then actually be a deterrent to learning.

If the content and methodology are suited to students' cognitive structures and styles, then it is likely that concepts and skills will be rapidly developed. Learning still requires effort by students, but if they can cope with problems and achieve mastery and a feeling of success, they are more likely to be motivated to learn and to enjoy school activities.

It is important for teachers to carefully observe their learners' actions and reactions to what they are called upon to do. An activity matched to one student's conceptual development could be too advanced for another. Individualization is essential in any classroom situation in which students are not homogeneously classified, as is the case in most classrooms.

Admittedly individualization requires developing new techniques and materials and an increased sensitivity on the part of teachers about utilizing these techniques and materials with individual learners. Individualization may more readily be achieved in a learning-by-doing, reality-centered environment.

We do not mean to imply that all education should be individualized. Group processes and interactions also play an important role in an individual's education. At the interpersonal level students are affected by the tone of the class—by the way teachers treat individual students, by various disciplinary measures, by excessive orderliness or disorderliness, by rigidities or flexibilities in implementing the curriculum, or by the ways teachers accept and support students' ideas, suggestions, and evaluations.[10] Respect by teachers for students begets respect by students for each other and feelings of openness, while disrespect tends to generate disrespect and feelings of subservience or hostility. Even the method of seating can affect attitudes toward teachers, the class, the school, and society.

Group communication provides a means of testing one's ideas and feelings and of learning how to correct one's misconceptions. One's view may be enlarged by the diversity of perceptions, feelings, and attitudes that may exist in a group about a given fact or

---

[10] Edmond P. Amidon and Ned A. Flanders. *The Role of the Teacher in the Classroom*, rev. ed. Association for Productive Teaching, 1040 Plymouth Building, Minneapolis, Minn. 55402, 1967.

issue. In the context of group or class activities democratic processes may be developed, strengthened, or weakened, and methods of making group decisions may be worked out. Group or whole class discussions are often essential for exchanging and clarifying ideas and conceptions. The main goal is to mix both individual and group or class approaches in reasonable balance.

STUDENT TUTORING

The most neglected educational resource for individualization in schools is the student body itself. It has been firmly established in a considerable number of schools at all levels that students are fully capable of providing meaningful instruction, particularly at a remedial level on a one-to-one basis.[11] Students receiving instruction are able to ask questions any time and receive immediate answers, a condition conducive to rapid progress, especially for those who are usually bewildered by what is going on in class.

Such individualized instruction can occur in many settings. A teacher faced with a wide range of abilities in one class can subdivide it into small groups and have more advanced students help the less advanced with prescribed activities. Arrangements may be made with another teacher of a class at a higher level for one-to-one tutoring by older students. Special tutoring squads may be organized among older students to work with younger children needing help during nonclass time or after school hours.

It is essential, of course, that tutors know more about the subject than the students being tutored, but the level need not be very much higher nor should it be assumed that only more advanced students make good tutors. In fact, so-called poor students, perhaps a few years older than those they are helping, can provide excellent tutoring services, as well as improve their own work.

A major factor in successful individualized tutoring programs is

---

[11] Alan Gartner et al. *Children Teach Children: Learning by Teaching.* New York: Harper & Row, 1971.

active participation and strong support by the school administration in organizing the program and providing suitable materials. Some teachers are strong enough to initiate and carry through programs in their own classes, but a large program requires administrative leadership.

Appropriate materials are important too because tutors require guidance in the specific instruction they offer. For remedial situations it is generally best to provide special instruction sheets for the tutor, either prepared by the school or purchased from commercial sources.[12]

Individualized, one-to-one tutoring by students is highly reality-centered. The abstract nature of a generalized thirty-to-one setting is eliminated, and the tutor and student interact on a natural, real, personal basis typical of most human relationships. The tutor works in a real-life setting that requires a high degree of responsibility, initiative, creative use of his intelligence, ingenuity, and use of all his communication skills. All of these qualities can greatly contribute to the success of individualized tutoring programs.

---

[12] A typical program of this kind, designed to teach reading by means of tutoring for nonreading teenagers, is the Hip Reader Program by C. Pollack and P. Lane, published by Book-Lab, Inc. Brooklyn, N.Y. 11218, 1970.

PATTERNS FOR
CHANGE

A number of aspects of traditional school organization and methodology impair the relationship of schooling to the real world. First and foremost school itself removes children and adolescents from the real world of home and work and places them in an artificial environment in separate buildings under the authority of a periodically changing group of adults. Young people are told where to go, where to sit, when to eat or go to the washroom, when they may stand up or leave the premises, and when they may talk (relatively rarely). If they already know what is being taught, they can't go off and do something else but must sit still and make believe that they are paying attention. If they find the work too complicated, they usually cannot stop the teacher and insist that their questions be answered.

Teachers are supposed to build into lesson plans some attention to individual differences, but, as a practical matter, this is generally very difficult to do for a class of thirty or so students who have a wide range of abilities. In essence, it is teachers who generally "do their thing" while students are passive, part-time listeners rather than active participants, followers rather than leaders, and watchers rather than doers. They wait for instructions, instead of initiating action, and they expect ideas to come from others, rather than originating thoughts for themselves.

In many cases students go home after school, plunk down in front of TV sets, and continue the role of watchers and listeners. Such a steady diet of "not learning by not doing" may be a major cause of the apathy many people exhibit toward the simple, everyday responsibilities expected of citizens. Student passivity and the narrow content of the subject-centered curriculum probably contribute to the atrophy of many skills, abilities, and values such as perseverance, independent thinking, flexibility, visualizing in three dimensions, relating to other people, and working cooperatively for common goals. Many educators and critics discern a loss of humaneness in the traditional school setting.

There is no hard scientific proof that the relatively rigid organizational structure of most school systems contributes to the effectiveness of learning. Indeed there is evidence to the contrary in the Eight Year Study, a controlled experiment conducted from 1932 to 1940 in thirty secondary schools.[1] A variety of programs, courses, and methods of instruction were offered to students, including reality-centered experiences that replaced traditional courses. Arrangements were made with accredited colleges to waive traditional rigid course requirements so that no student in the thirty schools would be penalized.

Evaluation of the entire program, which included completion of college study and beyond, revealed no significant differences in scholastic competence but instead substantial improvement in areas of personal and social responsibility, ability to work with

---

[1] W. M. Aiken, ed. *Story of the Eight Year Study*. New York: Harper & Row, 1942.

groups, and acquisition of democratic values—all of which tend to be neglected within a rigid, autocratic learning environment.

In addition to the inhumane effects of some aspects of the educational structure, the fact that a small percentage of teachers and supervisors are psychologically unsuited to work with students and exert a destructive, sometimes devastating influence in the inhumane way they handle young people must be resolutely faced. For example, one teacher, when complimented by a student teacher on the quiet and orderliness of her class, cheerfully confided her secret: "It's simple . . . At the beginning of the term, I destroy one child." What a price to pay! What justification would that teacher offer to the parents of that child?

The process of making schools more humane does not imply disorderliness as some may believe. The irresponsible freedom of students in some schools to disrupt the learning environment is equally unfair to all by destroying the possibility of effective learning. A humane school avoids both extremes of too rigid and too loose.

REALITY-CENTERED OPTIONS

Elements of a reality approach have always existed in some schools, in some courses, and in some classes taught by exceptional teachers. Many of the schools that participated in the previously mentioned Eight Year Study continued portions of the program on a permanent basis with realistic content and methodology and increased options and choices. These experiences provided numerous benefits in terms of personal and social development and work habits, without diminishing traditional academic standards.

Although the Eight Year Study ended in 1940, a significant number of secondary schools all over the nation (although a small minority of the total) have since converted to a similar organizational pattern. One such school is the Wilson Campus School at Mankato State College in Minnesota. A dominant feature of the

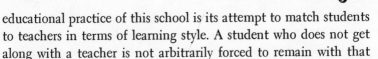

educational practice of this school is its attempt to match students to teachers in terms of learning style. A student who does not get along with a teacher is not arbitrarily forced to remain with that teacher, and suitable changes are made.

At the upper level students select the courses they want to take, a procedure that places poor courses at a competitive disadvantage and provides a strong incentive to make them up-to-date, reality-centered, and interesting. To some degree a teacher may be associated with a particular course and may be the main reason why a student chooses it or not. Variations in teaching styles usually correspond to the different learning styles of students so that there are generally enough students for most teachers, with some, of course, at the painful bottom of the heap. This unfortunate situation for a few teachers is hardly comparable to letting hapless students suffer the consequences of poor courses or teachers.

Schools that offer many options and choices for students are humane because they treat students in a mature, nonauthoritarian manner that is likely to be respected and to enlist their support and interest. Most schools of this type supplement their options with small group learning, team teaching, one-to-one remediation by student tutors, individual contact with teachers, less restrictive rules, and greater reliance on democratic peer pressures to provide a healthy learning environment. If enough of these schools are successful, this should guarantee that, over the long haul, their style of education will prevail generally.

Traditionally, vocational schools have attempted to apply a reality approach by gearing their curriculum to occupational goals such as automotive mechanics, aviation, food trades, fashion design, printing, and so on. Courses are supposed to integrate all the subject matter around a main theme. The degree of success, however, is very spotty, ranging from some excellent schools in which students with genuine interest in a subject are carefully selected and take high-level courses with reasonably integrated content, all the way to semi-prison schools that take the leftovers who have failed in the lower grades and halfheartedly try to breathe life into them with decrepit shops and equipment in dilapidated buildings.

An important trend on the reality-centered horizon is the specialized school based on an environmental theme. For example, the Beach Channel High School in New York City is located on the shores of Jamaica Bay and includes a dock, boats and ramps, indoor fish tanks, a scuba training pool, and laboratories for intensive scientific study of oceanography and sea life. A specially selected teaching staff meets regularly to develop integrated courses in which the major disciplines revolve around the central theme of oceanography. According to the principal, Robert L. Rappaport, "We're not replacing languages, literature, the arts, the sciences; we're enriching them. What we're trying to do is get kids excited about school."

In the math class students learn about graphs by plotting curves relating water temperature to salinity. Chemistry and biology students focus on the chemical and biological aspects of the sea. History classes include a large amount of ocean-related content, and English classes study the rich literature about the sea.

Integration of subject matter is still only partial, however, and the curriculum still is based to a considerable degree on the traditional subjects of English, history, art, math, and science. The full value of a reality approach will not be achieved until the traditional subjects become secondary and supplementary and not the prime focus of instruction. This is beginning to happen in schools such as Beach Channel, which offers courses on transportation and man and the sea. It will take a long time to accumulate the experience necessary to attain the fully integrated reality-centered content and methodology implied in such course titles, largely because these courses are taught by traditional science and social studies specialists who must undertake the difficult task of learning new content and modifying learning styles previously mastered.

An advanced example of reality-centered education is the Skyline Career Development Center in Dallas, Texas, which features facilities in buildings with fourteen acres of floor space on an eighty-four-acre campus. Inside the buildings are quantities of sophisticated technological equipment: an airplane hangar with eight airplanes and two helicopters, a color television studio, a one million dollar computer, a greenhouse, and twenty-eight career clusters, each focusing on a basic occupational area—arts, sciences, medical and dental professions, aeronautics, computer technology, fashion design and production, cosmetology, construction, landscaping, food services, and management.

In addition to the 3,600 students bused in every day from all parts of the city, a regular high school program with 1,000 students is conducted on the premises, and 4,000 adults attend courses at night as well as during the day. Academic study is not neglected and is woven into the curriculum; about half the time is devoted to such studies. Many students go on to college, while others go directly into jobs in industry made possible because of career training at the Center.

Besides the regular instructional staff, some 300 private citizens recruited by the Chamber of Commerce provide specialized instruction, give guest lectures, conduct and arrange field trips, help individual students find jobs, advise on the curriculum, help evaluate the performance of students and teachers, and obtain the use of equipment and manpower for the school as needed. The project is supported by local labor leaders who also offer special assistance.

One important outcome of this kind of reality approach is that the evils of homogeneous classes are minimized. Slow students in traditional academically oriented high schools usually find themselves segregated with other slow students in math, English, social studies, and biology classes. Rarely do they encounter average or superior students in their subject classes, except perhaps in the minor subjects of gym, music and art, or in homeroom. Moreover, if students are black, Puerto Rican, or Chicano, they are likely to be segregated into classes with all or mostly blacks, Puerto Ricans or Chicanos. Even where busing is used as a device to integrate schools, segregation may merely be transferred from the school as a whole to the classroom.

The career school concept reduces classroom and school segregation by offering a wide variety of reality-centered specialities. A black student is just as likely to specialize in aviation as a white student, and both are placed in the aviation shop where they are likely to reveal different kinds of aptitudes, to excel in different ways, and to be less stigmatized or stereotyped.

The extensive facilities, large range of reality instruction, and excellent reputation of the Skyline Career Development Center attract a wide range of students who are willingly bused in from all parts of the city. The composition of the school parallels the racial composition of the population: 64 percent white, 26 percent black, and 10 percent other minorities. Although this parallel may be deliberate, there are no typical segregation complaints because the school is a desirable place and whites want to go there as much as minorities do. Integration is by choice, not by compulsion.

The breadth, scope, and depth of its educational offerings lift the school well above the norm of the typical vocational school. The experiences accumulated in such schools in the next few years are bound to lead to significant new concepts and techniques for all schools. The basis for progress is sound, and with time this experimental approach, wholeheartedly supported by and involving all sections of the community, can improve the quality of instruction and the school's relationship to real life.

USEFUL WORK AS PART OF SCHOOLING

During the customary twelve years or more of schooling most students' time is spent preparing for some distant purpose that is usually never directly experienced. The explanation, "You will need this some day," is constantly repeated, but, for many, the need never arises.

The just described Skyline Career Development Center in Dallas has begun to experiment with useful work as an integral part of the school day. For example, students preparing for careers in construction actually build homes near the school, which are sold and the proceeds used to purchase materials for additional buildings and projects.

Anyone who has ever performed a carpentry job understands the sense of satisfaction obtained from cutting lumber to the right lengths and nailing the pieces in place. At the end of the day, one sees the results of one's work in the form of a wall, or a closet, or a built-in bookshelf. The sense of achievement is less concrete for traditional accomplishment in school—a talk, a set of papers, or a mark on a test. Just as young children must hold an object in their hands to obtain a feeling for its reality, so most young people need to make or build something to sense themselves as creators and doers. No doubt this accounts in some measure for the current tendency of many young people to leave school and take to the open spaces, build their own houses, and work at manual jobs.

A school that provides an outlet for this natural feeling to work on construction projects could make learning much more relevant. Mathematics and science are naturals for such projects. The process of preparing an order for lumber for the floors, walls, ceiling, and roof of a house involves many mathematical calculations, geometry, and algebra. The proper placement of a ridge beam for a sloping roof involves the geometry of the right triangle. Fitting beams and panels requires knowledge of measurement principles.

Science principles are constantly at work. For example, when using the notched end of a hammer to pull out a nail, it is often necessary to insert a block of wood under the hammer head to increase leverage and reduce the effort required. An explanation of why the task becomes easier entails a discussion of the laws of levers and the principle of the conservation of energy. The reason nails and screws have sharp points leads to a consideration of the principle of the wedge and how it relates to broader principles. The fact that a rectangular structure requires bracing with angled supports to form triangles leads to the study of the vector addition of forces. The installation of plumbing and heating systems could introduce many concepts of hydraulics and air and water pressure. The electrical system depends upon basic facts about circuitry, switching, conductivity, and insulation.

Keeping a record of costs involves elementary bookkeeping and accounting. Style, design, and decoration involve many art concepts. Writing instructions for other students and reading books about construction involve language skills. History and anthropology may be brought in by researching the many types of shelter man has developed in the past.

The rising costs of lumber can be related to economic forces as well as diminishing timber resources. How do practices of clear cutting of national forests, lack of provision for planting trees, selling American lumber to foreign markets, and the increasing use of paper affect the lumber supply and needs? Answers to such questions involve ecology, conservation, economics, politics, and international relations.[2]

This type of integrated education implies more and better planning at all levels and team teaching as well as outside instructional resources. Teachers must have a much wider range of skills than at present and understand that it is natural for most men and women—and better for them and for society—to learn to work with their hands as well as with their brains.

More experimentation should be undertaken in every school. Teaching techniques and skills would then be developed on the job—a kind of reality training project for teachers. One feasible way to begin is for students to build camps or recreation centers in their communities with all students devoting some time to such activities as part of his or her schooling.

Work-study programs in which students work at part-time jobs while they go to school have been tried for decades. In the main these have involved students at the lower end of the academic

2 See Peter Harnik's "Logging in Alaska," *Environmental Action*, September 1, 1973, pp. 9–12.

ladder who would leave school if it did not offer some work experience. With Sputnik and the acceleration of science and math training, some older, upper level students have been given opportunities to work as laboratory helpers in summer institutes.

In general, experiences with work-study programs have been positive at all levels. Students relate to the reality of work experiences and begin to identify their interests with the school program, especially if their courses are related to the work they do. Specially trained teachers are generally required to integrate studies with the actual work students perform. In an ideal program teachers would be made thoroughly familiar with the jobs, and courses and teaching materials would be matched with the work performed.

One of the most important functions of a work-study program is to provide students with career and employment guidance. Personal experiences and observations in places of employment give some indication of the kinds of work they might like to do as adults. Equally important is the experience of useful, gainful employment itself. Many young people suffer traumatic shocks when they leave school and have to go out to work. Even a small percentage of time spent in places of employment, under school control, beginning at about age fourteen would help ease the transition to the world of work for many young people who don't make that transition now.

Despite the definite value of work-study programs, support at the governmental level is halfhearted or less. School people themselves generally scrounge around and beg for jobs for their students. Employers just do not want to be bothered training inexperienced young people; it often costs more to train them than their actual accomplishments on the job are worth. Some schools have arranged jobs with other public institutions such as hospitals and libraries, either on a nonpaying basis or with small stipends the institution can afford to pay.

The reality of work related to study is so important that it would be in the best interests of the nation to support work-study programs for all students on a regular, planned basis beginning as early as the eighth or ninth grade. Subsidies or tax incentives could be offered to public agencies and private enterprises that organize work for young people. The combination of work accomplished on the job plus subsidy or tax advantages would eventually outweigh the specific costs to a company of starting and maintaining a program with appropriate standards.

It would be best for students to have a variety of jobs in different places during their school years so that they would be able to compare the opportunities available. They would also realize the variety of skills required in the outside world and be stimulated to master the academic aspects of their schoolwork. Instruction related to the jobs should show students how various skills are utilized in the industries in which they might work. Programs should include discussions about such questions with both employees and management.

These objectives require organizing work-study programs on national, state, and local levels, with considerable cooperative planning and financial support, but such efforts would be economically productive because young people would be more effectively guided, trained, and integrated into the world of work.

ROLE OF THE COMMUNITY

The open classroom concepts developed in the British infant schools have spurred the development of experimental reality-centered counterparts at the secondary level in the United States, whose philosophical roots go back to John Dewey's learning-by-doing ideas. In effect, the walls of the traditional school begin to disappear, and the learning process moves outward into the entire community.

This new trend is part of a long-range movement for integrating the community into the educational process—a return to the community's original role as the educational fountainhead. As Ralph Tyler puts it:

In most if not all societies, children and youth learn more of the behavior important for constructive participation in the society outside of school than within. This fact does not diminish the importance of school but underlines the nation's dependence on the home, the working place, the community institutions, the peer group, and other informal experiences to furnish a major part of the education required for a child to be successfully inducted into society. Only by clear recognition of the school's special responsibilities can it be highly effective in educating its students.[3]

There are many aspects to school-community involvement, ranging from the all too familiar confrontation over school policies, particularly busing and integration, to the opening of school doors for adult education and to parents and school volunteers to participate as teaching helpers. For the purpose of this book—reality-centered learning—the principal potential of the community is as an educational resource or as a place for learning.

One of the pioneers of the school-without-walls movement is the Parkway Program High School in Philadelphia, which does not have a school building of its own. Most classes are conducted in museums, art galleries, government offices, factories, social welfare facilities, health centers, colleges, and any other out-of-school facilities students may be investigating. Three self-governing communities composed of teachers and students determine policies and programs at weekly town meetings. Here students discuss with the staff what they want to learn, and teachers then suggest ways of obtaining that knowledge. Specialists are called upon to offer guidance and instruction—a reporter discusses journalism on the premises of a newspaper; a jeweler offers instructions on gemcutting; a health worker discusses problems of health care at a local medical center. Instruction in standard subjects such as

---

[3] In "Some Optimism Justified" by Alan C. Purvis, *New York Times Annual Education Review*, January 16, 1974, p. 74. Ralph W. Tyler, former Dean of the School of Education at the University of Chicago, has been called the "dean of modern curriculum thinking."

math or English is offered at two-hour sessions twice a week.[4]

In some schools of this kind students may complete one course requirement by working for a period of time as an aide in a congressman's office, where they obtain an insider's knowledge of how the political process works. Other students may do a stint of manual work by helping to restore an old sawmill or serve as a guide in a museum. A group of students may work at a local government office handling complaints from consumers. Others may study the courts by observing actual trials or spend several days a week for a few months helping out in a nursery school. Still others may take advanced courses at colleges in the area. To prevent overspecialization and to provide a range of experiences, each student takes a variety of short courses during the year.

In some cases students are intimately involved in planning and other operational phases of the school. Committees of students may interview applicants for the school; others may perform tasks in the maintenance and daily operation of the school.

In addition to the regular staff, teachers of special courses may be recruited from the community. One mini-course may be taught once a week by an insurance broker, an artist may give a course in his studio, or a playwright may help to develop a student play.

There are no grades, but credits for courses are assigned, or not, on the basis of actual accomplishment. Evaluation is based on teachers' recommendations, the daily logs students keep, and the reports they write on their experiences.

One of the obvious pluses for such schooling is the high degree of student motivation. Students generally clamor to be admitted to such schools, with more applicants than can be accommodated.

Of course, such radical departures from traditional schooling create many problems. The question, "But can students read and write?" is crucial. How much mathematics and history will they miss? If the pendulum swings too far toward the outside world, it may be necessary to backtrack and balance real-life courses with

---

[4] I. Ezra Staples. "The Open Space Plan in Education," *Educational Leadership*, February 1971, pp. 458–60.

some academic minima. But the overall direction is healthy and long overdue. Nothing but good can come from the experience of breaking out of the encrusted traditional mold and undertaking experimental programs such as reality-centered schools without walls. No doubt, in time, this movement will seep into the regular schools and break down a few more walls, even if not all.

REALITY TRAINING OF TEACHERS

Many beginning teachers, their heads full of theoretical concepts but with little contact with real students, are suddenly plunged into a classroom to sink or swim on their own. Some are so unprepared for what they find that they quickly leave the profession. Most eventually manage to achieve competence and expertise, but only after an unnecessarily difficult and sometimes long and painful period of adjustment.

Over the years, teacher education institutions have gradually increased the time that prospective teachers spend with students and actual classroom problems, but the allotted time is still not enough. One reality-centered approach in a performance-based program at Brooklyn College of the City University of New York begins with tutoring students of different ages in various subjects (math, English, science) in one-to-one or small group situations, under the direct supervision of a college faculty member whose job it is to relate theory to reality. Subsequent classroom discussion of educational and psychological theory takes on much greater meaning in the context of prior contact with real students and problems. The individualized supervision in this program is geared to help prospective teachers recognize their strengths and identify and correct their weaknesses in a one-to-one relationship that improves their self-confidence and performance.[5]

---

[5] See *Performance-Based Undergraduate Program for Education of Teachers at Brooklyn College,* edited by N. Darcy. A Curriculum Document published by the School of Education, Brooklyn College, City University of New York, 1971.

Another reality-centered approach used at Fairleigh Dickinson University, Rutherford, New Jersey, is three-month bus tours for prospective teachers in which the entire class visits schools and community educational programs in a number of states to obtain firsthand experience with a variety of teaching situations and methods. The tour also provides a career guidance function— prospective teachers get a close look at the variety of teaching jobs available in different places in the country.

Increased contact and work with students in classrooms are crucial in helping prospective teachers learn that the quality of the teacher-student relationship shapes not only student attitudes but also achievements. A recent report by the Fleischmann Commission, surveying educational policy in New York State, found that student attitudes toward school were heavily influenced by their perceptions of the teacher and the climate of learning in the classroom.[6] It is also interesting to note that teachers were unaware of students' feelings and interests in discussing moral, political, and personal issues—the reality aspects of subject content.

Major changes in teacher education may be expected in the years to come. One probable change is the blending of teacher education with school and community programs so that theory is taught in a manner completely integrated with the realities teachers actually face. Such changes will involve reassessment and continuous updating of a teacher's knowledge and skills through informal and formal inservice education at teaching-learning centers as is now proposed and under development in the United States or as in the presently operating British teacher center models.[7] The centers offer teachers opportunities to exchange information, attend workshops and seminars, evaluate new programs and teacher

---

[6] *Fleischmann Report on the Quality, Cost, and Financing of Elementary and Secondary Education in New York State*, 3 vols. New York: Viking Press, 1973.

[7] Ben Rosner. *The British Teacher Center: A Report on Its Development, Current Operations, Effects and Applicability to Teacher Education in the United States*. New York: Office of Teacher Education, City University of New York, November 1972.

roles, and to obtain help in implementing new ideas. In the course of such activities, teachers seek and accept changes in methods to evaluate their teaching competence. A recent poll of teachers indicates a majority expect their performance to be evaluated by administrators, teachers, students, and parents.[8] Other aspects of evaluating teachers' competence may include the performance of their students and a periodic inservice assessment of knowledge, skills and attitudes.[9]

---

[8] "Survey of Scholastic Institute of Teacher Opinion," *Scholastic Teacher*, January 1974.

[9] *New Directions in Preparing Teachers: A Position Paper for the Regents of the University of the State of New York*. Albany, N.Y. : State Education Department, March 1972.

DEVELOPING REALITY-CENTERED TOPICS AND MINICOURSES

Movements for curriculum change have accelerated in recent years partially as a consequence of Sputnik, which spawned national curriculum committees in science and mathematics and more recently in other subjects. Most of these new trends have emphasized reality content and deal with current issues and sensory involvement, particularly through laboratory activities and, in some instances, community participation. Key ideas, basic skills, processes and strategies for learning, and integration of subjects—all characteristics of a reality approach—are also stressed. The following areas of study of some new programs indicate the extent of the direction of change toward reality and integration of subject matter: life cycles, populations, environments, communities, ecosystems, structural functions, senses, behavior, learning, demography, human ecology, impact of technology, traffic flow, computers, communications, automation, energy, environment, and social values. Many abstract concepts involving such characteristics of the real world are included such as factors limiting growth, change, balance, diversity, complexity, stability, interactions, systems, variables, and reference frames and models are more helpful for understanding today's reality than former subject matter such as the War of 1812 or Euclid's thirty-first proposition. Most of the new courses are in the mainstream and are flexible, reality-related topics and minicourses. Many of the concepts referred to have been developed in special programs. Some of these programs are listed at the end of this chapter.

Developments in the British infant schools in the postwar period of 1946 to the present gave impetus to this minicourse movement. Although at first this movement involved only the lower elementary grades, the thrust of its philosophy and methodology has been seeping into upper elementary grades and is beginning to penetrate secondary school levels. One interesting development has been the use of "topics" to introduce reality into learning. Unlike the limited meaning of the word in the older methodology, the sense of the word "topic" as adapted from the British model is considerably broader and much more flexible. A topic is a special study by an individual, group, or class of a subject of interest to the students and is developed by them with the use of any and every educational tool at their disposal—even outside the classroom or the school, if necessary and if possible. The degree to which a topic cuts across subject matter lines will depend on individual or group interest.

In the course of investigating a topic students may engage in a wide assortment of instructional experiences. For example, activities could include planning and implementing logical methods of inquiry such as how to check hypotheses or where to find data as well as direct instruction from a teacher in the use of library catalogs or the rules for punctuation. A topic at the secondary level is also open-ended in time; it may be pursued as long as it is capable of serving as the basis for further study—for a week, a month, or even over a period of years if a student desired to do so on his own.

Such flexible reality-centered topics conflict with traditional courses with fixed content specified by a series of lessons or units or old-fashioned topics. The basic problem for teachers in schools with traditional courses is, "How can I include reality-centered topics in the particular courses I teach?" For the supervisor the equivalent problem is altering a school's organization to allow time for topics and minicourses. Modular scheduling and independent study are two ways of providing more flexibility in the school day and encouraging teachers to include minicourses in their teaching.

DEVELOPING TOPICS

The simplest way to develop a new topic is to adopt one developed by a curriculum committee in one's subject area. These are generally accompanied by booklets and teachers' guides that provide good background for both student and teacher reference.[1] A related method is to borrow and adapt a completed unit, and perhaps even the materials, from a colleague. This kind of teacher exchange can be a major source of new topics and should be encouraged by supervisors.

Another method relies upon the personal experiences of students. A local robbery could trigger an investigation of crime and the systems of controlling it—police, courts, and prisons. If a classmate is confined in a hospital, this could spark a study of medicine and health care. If students pay a high price for sporting equipment, the class may be interested in investigating the causes of inflation. Noxious fumes from a nearby factory smokestack or superhighway could initiate the topic of air pollution. If there is

---

[1] A series of pamphlets dealing with topics of current interest is available from Xerox Education Publications, Education Center, Columbus, Ohio, 43216.

immediate, personal contact with a problem, it is concrete, real, and more stimulating than a remote generalized problem.

Still another way of initiating a topic is to use special competencies of students. A student who is a photography bug could lead an investigation of that topic. Another who is a space flight enthusiast could serve as the central resource for a study of space. A teacher should seek to discover these special skills, perhaps through general discussion or from compositions keyed to elicit information about students' interests and competencies. Some interests may be difficult to unearth because students do not think they are suitable for a school situation or don't think them applicable, for example, fashion design or jazz or rock music.[2] If teachers are alert to opportunities, they can generate topics that give student experts feelings of self-worth. Students who present their area of expertise in an organized fashion may develop new ideas and enlarge their view and may transmit enough enthusiasm to interest others in the same topic.

A topic takes on added reality if it creates opportunities for decision-making.[3] For example, if a local beach is so badly polluted that students cannot swim at it, the topic of water pollution might be studied with the purpose of gathering information that will lead to a corrective plan to present to local or state authorities. Such a project involves research, investigation, and use of interpersonal and communication skills in the political process.

An ambitious project of this kind, which some classes have carried through, involves the following steps: *1*) identifying the

[2] Some teachers may wonder about the wisdom of including a topic such as jazz or rock music. Actually, the best examples of these musical forms have a degree of excellence likely to give them permanent cultural status. The best songs of the Beatles, Simon and Garfunkel, and Bob Dylan are in the idiom of our time and express the human condition as well as any songs of the past. An alert teacher of English, music, or social studies could make good use of recordings of songs to generate very interesting reality lessons about today's world.

[3] Student and teacher materials for a unit on "Decision-making" are available from Scholastic Book Services, Englewood Cliffs, N.J. 07632.

problem, 2) collecting pertinent information, including history, technical data, and laboratory testing, 3) listing possible solutions, 4) evaluating solutions in terms of feasibility and possible action, 5) planning a strategy for action, 6) taking action, 7) evaluating the effectiveness of the actions, and 8) possibly redefining the problem and adjusting actions to fit new situations encountered. The process can be most effective in developing attitudes, values, beliefs, and appreciations as well as concepts. Projects of this kind can be interwoven with a series of topics in a minicourse or regular course on environmental problems—air and water pollution, garbage disposal or noise pollution, for instance.

Side issues always arise in any reality-centered topic and can easily be expanded into major investigations. For example, in the process of studying air pollution questions are likely to arise about the relative merits of air pollution controls on cars and other engines. Most of these devices waste fuel and reduce gasoline mileage, severely offsetting their advantages. It is not possible for students to resolve such highly technical matters, but it is useful for them to realize that judgments must often be withheld until more information is available.

Reality-centered topics may be easily generated from real events described in newspaper reports, magazine articles, TV news programs, and documentaries. If a topic is reality-related, it will, sooner or later, appear in the news. For example, consider the following article about cold and colds:

Cold Unrelated To Colds

Of all the beliefs about cold, none is more persistent than the one that says it brings on the common cold.

Well, then, what will happen to homeowners who do what PRESIDENT NIXON has asked and turn their thermostats down six degrees, to achieve a national average of 68 degrees? And to workers whose employers lower temperatures 10 degrees in compliance with new government regulations?

Doctors say living in a cooler environment will not make you more susceptible to colds.

DR. BILL BARCLAY, the American Medical Association's spokesman for scientific affairs, says it is actually healthier for people to live with temperatures in the upper 60s. "When you warm cold air, you dry it out," he says. "And extreme dryness in the air aggravates respiratory problems."

Moreover, Barclay says, there is no evidence, contrary to popular belief, that chilling the body makes one more vulnerable to virus attacks. To test this, doctors at Baylor University (Tex.) College of Medicine inoculated two groups of volunteers with a cold virus. Then they put one group in a warm room and the other in a room cooled to 40 degrees. The number who caught colds were about the same in each group.

It is true that more persons get colds in winter than in summer. But the researcher at Baylor says that people are indoors far more often during the winter and in closer proximity. Colds, they say, come not from low temperatures but from persons who already have colds and are spreading cold viruses.

Although cold temperatures will not give a healthy person a cold, it may aggravate other physical conditions.

LUCY KAVALER, author of the book, "Freezing Point," and an expert on cold temperatures, says that the cold can reduce the flow of blood in the peripheral vessels. This makes cold particularly hazardous for persons with some heart conditions. "A man who is able to climb stairs easily in the summer may suffer a mild attack when doing the same thing in winter," she said.

But, she adds, it is doubtful that a four- or six-degree change could bring on this reaction. A study by the National Heart Institute showed that moderate exercise begins to be troublesome for angina patients when the temperature reaches 59 degrees.

However, if a limited drop in the thermostat is not apt to

affect health, that is not to say it will not affect comfort. "Reduction of two degrees probably would not be noticeable," says Dr. Frederick H. Rohles, director of Kansas State University's Institute for Environmental Research. "But a reduction of six degrees probably would be objectionable."[4]

The general topic might be classified as cold or colds, but the content of the article suggests the following subtopics and questions for investigation:

Cold: What is heat? What is cold? What would happen to the earth and to people if the sun stopped shining and the earth cooled off? How do Americans express temperature? How do Europeans express temperature? How can we convert temperatures on our scale to theirs?

Conserving Energy: Why do government officials advocate lowering house temperatures? What measures can people take to conserve heat and energy? How did people conserve energy in the past? (Ask the old folks.)

Health: What is a cold? How did the cold (disease) get its name? What causes colds? What effect does lower temperature have on catching a cold? Why do people have more colds in winter? Do drafts cause colds? (Ask at home; then ask a doctor.) How do you handle the previous investigation to avoid antagonizing those who think cold causes colds? What effect does cold air have on people with heart conditions? What is angina? How is health related to humidity? What are the causes of respiratory diseases? What is a virus? Are viruses more likely to infect the body in cold weather? What harm can excessive cold do?

Humidity: What is dry air? Humid air? Why does heating the air lower the humidity? What effect does low humidity have on the body? High humidity?

Comfort: What temperature is most comfortable? (Investigate with friends and neighbors.) How is humidity related to comfort?

---

[4] Used by permission of Fort Myers News-Press.

How can people become accustomed to colder temperatures? (Try it out yourself.)

EXPERIMENTS: How can doctors show that cold air does not cause a cold or increase infection from viruses causing colds? What is a controlled experiment? Was the experiment described in the article a controlled experiment? If the experiment had not been controlled, would it have proved anything? Why?

HISTORY OF MAN: Find out how the men at Valley Forge survived the cold during the winter. How did very early man survive in the winter? How do Eskimos manage to live in temperatures that would kill most of us? How did the Ice Age affect man's history? It is thought that no people lived in North America before about 11,000 years ago. How did they get here? In what way is this history related to the Ice Age and cold climates?

This extensive list was generated from one newspaper article. There is enough intellectual meat here for a minicourse that cuts across a spectrum of customary academic subjects, with possible concept developments diverging in many fruitful directions. The same method of generating questions may be applied to any informative news item or article. Students should assume major responsibility for answering the questions by library research, experiments, or other investigative means involving the entire gamut of skills in learning how to learn. Verbal and written communication or displays should be an integral part of the activity. Understanding mathematical relationships should be encouraged, i.e., the conversion of Fahrenheit degrees to Celsius (centigrade).

TECHNIQUES AND FACILITIES

The general approach for teaching topics is somewhat different from the customary convergent approach to subject studies. The methodology focuses around learning-by-doing, teaching young people how to learn, and developing decision-making and investigative abilities. The role of the teacher is basically that of an organizer who selects problems of interest to students, helps them to plan an attack on the problems, and provides suitable materials and guidance to enable them to make satisfying progress. Without such organization, investigations of topics are likely to be haphazard, with maximum time-wasting and minimum accomplishment.

Teachers need not feel obligated to know all the facts about a topic, although it is helpful if they are at least reasonably conversant with them. They should do at least a modest amount of reading about it in advance. Alert teachers will learn from the students, especially the first few times a topic is studied. Knowledge and competence with a topic will grow each time it is presented for investigation. Eventually, teachers will develop a repertory of topics that they should try to keep up-to-date with current information and new sources and by pruning old materials.

A group of teachers will have a much wider range of skills and abilities than any one in the group. Each can serve as a resource for the special skills he or she possesses or acquires. If a teacher who has no mathematical skills is advising students who want to investigate population growth mathematically, it would be much more effective to refer them to another teacher with mathematical expertise. Even where team teaching is not formalized, cooperation may be effectively developed on an informal basis, especially where encouraged by supervisors. The rigid time structure of the school day, with definite periods for specific subjects, interferes with such exchange of skills and resources, but this obstacle may be minimized by allotting specific times during the school day or week for conferences.

Upper-level students may act as advisers or lecturers about aspects of a topic, relieving the teacher of the burden of answering difficult questions that inevitably arise in a reality-centered topic. For example, the teacher of a fourth-grade class in Michigan City, Indiana, who developed an earth science unit, obtained assistance from students in an advanced science class at a neighboring high school who answered special questions asked by the children.[5] Among the questions were: "How did they find out that the earth moves rather than the sun?" and "Water that goes into the ground sinks in; how about the lakes? Why doesn't it sink in there?"

Preparing answers to these difficult questions proved to be a real challenge to the advanced science students and involved not only research and investigation on their own but full utilization of many communication skills. These students benefitted while, at the same time, they performed a useful service as supplementary educators of younger children. Teachers who are not experts in a given topic will feel more confident presenting them if student experts from high school and college levels are available for consultation and special "lectures."

Another critical aspect of offering topics is the development of more effective library materials and research facilities in schools. If reading is to be encouraged and used as a skill in carrying on investigations, then suitable reference materials must be available at the students' levels. Schools generally attempt to meet this need with textbooks, encyclopedic compendia of all that students are supposed to know about a given subject at their level. But textbooks, although they may serve some useful functions, are simply too limited in scope and too rigid to provide all the needs of reality-centered learning, particularly in a rapidly changing society where what one needs to know changes so quickly.

The local library and school library are also generally not adequately prepared to service a fully reality-centered educational system. A teacher who needs a set of maps of the local area going back to early colonial days is not likely to obtain them in the school library. A ninth-grade student who wants to study Chinese customs is not likely to be able to cull through a number of books to pick out occasional passages that may apply. A student who wishes to make a photographic display will not find an enlarger or photographic equipment in most schools.

---

[5] George Hultgren. "Heterogeneous Age Grouping Today," *Science Teacher*, March 1974, p. 37.

School media centers, sometimes developing from or combined with libraries or science laboratories, are increasingly being developed to provide the varied materials required by reality-centered topics.[6] As teachers develop topics over a period of time, they can simultaneously arrange to store their resource materials —books, pamphlets, clippings, photographs, filmstrips, movies, and student reports—in the centralized media center. Reports by other teachers of their experience with specific topics could also provide guidance.

Although a reality-centered topics approach involves shifting from rigidly centralized to decentralized methods and greater responsibility for supervisors and teachers, this does not mean that central authorities can abrogate their responsibilities. If anything, their responsibility for providing leadership and assistance to teachers increases. For example, a large central educational authority, such as that for a large city or state, could develop facilities and resource centers to serve large numbers of schools. A request from a teacher or from a school for materials and suggestions for a project on ancient Mexican history, or causes of inflation, or overpopulation should, within a few days, be answered with a packet of materials for developing a study of the topic. Such a service could effectively use computers and rapid inexpensive printing and photocopying equipment which are too expensive and inefficient for individual schools.

Resource centers of this kind are already effectively operating in various school systems. The school systems of Fairfax, Virginia, and North Dakota have developed outstanding examples of such centers, and the trend is spreading.

It is of considerable importance that the reading level of the materials be somewhere within the grasp of the involved youngsters. It is good practice to provide ninth graders with standard newspaper clippings and magazine articles. If these are moderately above their reading level, they will manage to dig out useful in-

---

[6] Ruth Ann Davies, ed. *School Library Media Center: A Force for Educational Excellence*, 2nd ed. New York: R. R. Bowker, 1974.

formation, and the reading will build vocabulary and language skills. But there would be little point in giving such materials to most readers at the fourth-grade level; in fact, the net effect would probably be negative and discourage future attempts to investigate problems.

Students should be encouraged to work together and share experiences when doing research on topics. Student "experts" in the class with different competencies can serve as resource persons. Worthwhile reports by previous students may be filed as references, performing the double function of giving meaning and usefulness to students' work and guidance for other students.

Adequate instruction in the use of research facilities is essential. Students should learn how to use the dictionary, the encyclopedia, the card catalog in the library, and special references and indexes such as the *Readers' Guide*. They should learn how to operate equipment such as photocopying machines, filmstrip and movie projectors, taping equipment, electric typewriters, and photographic equipment.

Naturally, no one expects such facilities and competencies to be developed all at once. The main thing is to begin where one can and gradually build up resources and know-how by actual doing. Within a decade, or two, or three, educational methodology could be transformed into a reality-centered approach.

AN EXAMPLE: THE TOPIC OF TREES

Consider the topic of trees, which was motivated by the following statements in a class discussion:

North Africa, along the Mediterranean Sea (locate sea and adjacent countries on a map) was covered with vast areas of forests thousands of years ago. Today most of this area is uninhabitable desert. Find out how this change occurred.

Investigation by students and discussion revealed several possible causes for the change. First, people inhabiting that area followed the common practice of clearing the forest by burning it, and when grass grew, the land was used for grazing sheep and goats. But these animals, unlike cattle, crop the grass so closely that it is eventually destroyed if grazing is too intensive. This exposes the soil to the wind, which blows it away, leaving bare rock and sand that can no longer support plant growth. Ultimately, if the area received little rain, a desert formed. It is believed that this was one process that fostered the growth of deserts in North Africa.

Another factor was changing climate produced by altered wind and rainfall patterns. As recently as January 28, 1974, the *New York Times* reported southward enlargement of the Sahara Desert at a rate of thirty miles per year because of a southward shift of the monsoon winds.

Such an introduction offers many possible directions for student investigations that cut across many disciplines. They can pursue the following:

Imagine that there were no trees. How would the earth be different from what it is today?

A termite can live by feeding on dry wood. Why doesn't man use wood to manufacture food? What research is being done in this area? Would it be important if a breakthrough could be made in this investigation? Could leaves be used for food?

Could trees help solve the fuel crisis? Could vehicles operate on fuel produced from trees? (Occasional photographs of cars operated by wood-burning furnaces that produce gas have appeared in newspapers.)

How is coal related to trees? (investigate fossils)

What is the connection between oil in the ground and trees?

How could man survive if there were no trees?

What uses of wood do you find in your home?

Investigate how various materials such as paper, plastic, fibers, and chemicals are made from trees.

Can you make some paper from wood?

In many parts of the world people depend on charcoal as their heat source for cooking. Find out about different methods of making charcoal and try to make some charcoal to cook a simple meal.

How does man farm trees?

What are some of the ecological precautions man must take when he cuts down trees?

What is the relationship between trees and soil?

What is the relationship between trees and floods?

If someone has cut down a tree recently, determine its age by counting the number of rings. Take a photograph of the rings and analyze it to find out what happened to the tree in the past. (Closely spaced rings indicate poor growth and little rainfall; distorted rings may be due to bending.) A local lumber mill, woodsman, or a parent may cooperate by cutting a series of thin sections from different trees or branches that may then be studied by students in class. (These sections could range from three to twelve inches in diameter and one-half to one or two inches thick.)

How old is the oldest tree? How do anthropologists and archeologists use tree rings to date ancient civilizations? How can they determine the climate in the past?

Plant seeds from apples, pears, oranges, lemons, grapefruits, peaches, or plums in pots and observe and record their growth.

What types of trees grow on your block and in your neighborhood? Learn how to identify them from the general shape, arrangement of branches, leaves, height, bark, and other characteristics.

Make a detailed study of leaves of different trees. How do the veins branch? What is the general shape? Are the edges smooth or notched?

What causes leaf color to change in the fall? What colors do you observe for different types of trees?

What trees besides sugar maples produce sweet sap in the spring? Try taking syrup from different kinds of trees.

Why do some city trees die?

Why are the trees along a road with heavy traffic not as healthy as those on a street with little traffic?

How do street lights, especially the orange-yellow sodium lights, affect the health of trees?

How many trees must be cut every year to make the paper for one of the newspapers in your area? (One ton of paper requires approximately seventeen trees.)

How many trees are needed to supply the paper used by your class for a year? By the school?

What are some of the ways the use of trees could be reduced for lumber, paper, chemicals, and plastics?

How are trees related to animal life?

What would happen if the supply of trees in the United States became exhausted?

No doubt every teacher could add other activity-generating questions to this list, and students themselves will come up with their own ideas, once they are started on an investigatory path.

TOPICS OF MAJOR INTEREST

Although the number of possible topics that might be explored is vast, it is essential to select those that are most likely to fulfill educational goals. Perhaps the most fruitful general areas today are studies of the environment from a broad viewpoint in which social, economic, and political factors are integrated with science, mathematics, and art. One major aspect of this vital subject, the impossibility of continuous growth, will be discussed in detail in chapter 10. Additional topics related to the social and physical environment that could easily be incorporated into existing or special courses are:

The Energy Crisis

What would the world be like today if we were deprived of all modern sources of energy—oil, gas, coal, electricity, and nuclear reactors?

What is meant by energy?

What caused the current energy crisis?

How rapidly has use of energy been growing? Could such growth continue forever?

What sources of energy are nonpolluting?

In what ways are industrial growth related to increased use of energy?

Which requires more energy to produce: aluminum or steel? nylon or cotton? plastics or wood? How are the answers to these questions related to the energy crisis?

What manufactured materials are biodegradable? What does that term mean?

How do production and transportation of military materials contribute to the energy crisis?

What types of human activity require very little commercial energy? Which activities use large quantities? (One trip by plane across the ocean uses as much fuel per passenger as if each passenger drove his own large car the same distance.)

How much energy per person do Americans use compared with people in other countries? Can this rate of consumption be continued?

Are nuclear power plants of the type now available the answer to energy problems? Why?

Investigate the use of hydrogen as a fuel for industry, cars, and home electricity. Why is it much less polluting than other fuels?

Should fuel be rationed or should demand be curbed by price increases? What other plans might be considered?

How will the energy crisis affect our life style? Sports? Auto racing? Use of boats and yachts? Airplane travel? Cultural and liesure activities?

What effects will a fuel shortage have on employment? Wages? Taxes?

How can injustices in allocating fuel be avoided?

How might replacing gas car engines with electric motors run by batteries ease the fuel shortage?

Pollution[7]

The following general questions apply to each of the major forms of pollution—air, water, solid waste disposal, noise, and others. These should be treated separately but in relation to each other where possible.

What are the basic causes of pollution today?

Did cavemen have any pollution problems?

How do pollutants cause damage?

Trace the history of a pollutant from the time it was introduced to the present. (DDT is a good example.)

How are pollutants detected?

What are the effects on health?

What are the economic effects?

How does the concentration of people in cities contribute to pollution?

How does industry cause pollution?

How do consumers cause pollution?

What can be done to curb pollution?

How can economic growth be maintained without increasing the use of energy?

How and why are developing countries affected by energy shortages in the industrial countries?

What new sources and forms of energy should be investigated (solar energy, geothermal energy, oil shale, Gulf Stream, tides, wind, alcohol from wood, hydrogen, or others)?

How is energy related to the economy?

How do economic incentives, such as the oil depletion allowance, affect availability of energy?

How may energy shortages be artificially produced or intensified to raise prices?

How does the possession of huge energy reserves by nonindustrial nations affect national and international politics?

---

[7] A unit "Environment," part of the Contact Series, is published by Scholastic Book Services, Englewood Cliffs, N.J. 07632.

What role do multinational companies play in the production, sale, and allocation of oil supplies?

How much has already been done to stop pollution? What can you do?

What will be the economic and social costs of curbing pollution?

What role can recycling play?

What changes in life style will be necessary to stop pollution? Apply this to the use of cars.

How can pollution problems be alleviated by new energy sources or ways of producing goods?

How are pollution problems handled in spaceships?

Technology [8]

What is meant by technology? Give some examples.

Why do engines tend to replace men and animals as sources of power? (See discussion of cost of electricity in chapter 10.)

What was the Industrial Revolution? How did it come about?

Some people think a new kind of technological revolution based on electronics and computers is taking place. What is the evidence for this judgment?

A ten dollar radio today is better than a hundred dollar radio of forty years ago, despite inflation. How did this enormous improvement occur?

Investigate an industry and find out how it manufactures its products. Local industries are best for such studies since field trips or visits by students are practicable. A good industry to study is printing because schools usually have relationships with printers, and newspapers are likely to cooperate.

---

[8] The Educational Development Center in Newton, Massachusetts, has developed a unit, "Man in a Man-made World," which deals mainly with technology. The New Jersey Department of Education has developed a unit "Technology for Children," which provides useful information. A more recent set of curriculum materials entitled "Technology ⟷ Environment" has been designed by the Engineering Concepts Curriculum Project (College of Engineering, State University of New York at Stony Brook, New York 11790) for secondary students who have not been successful academically.

Many ancient civilizations had developed technologies. Investigate the state of technology of an ancient civilization such as that of Egypt at the time of the building of the pyramids. Are there any technologies of former times from which we can learn something of value for solving problems today? For example, ancient technology made extensive use of wind power in windmills and sailboats and obtained energy from wheels moved by water.

How did the people in ancient Britain move the gigantic stones to Stonehenge? How did the people of Easter Island move similar large stones?

What is meant by technological assessment? Why is it important to make assessments of the future effects of new technologies?

How might the harmful effects of automobiles on society have been avoided?

What new technologies should be encouraged by new research?

Every new technology has good and bad effects. Select one area of technology for study and show these trade-offs. (For example, electronic amplifiers produce pleasure for some but noise pollution for others. Many musicians and listeners suffer hearing loss. An investigation of actual hearing loss of students in the school could be undertaken.) What recommendations would you make for minimizing harmful effects?

How has technology contributed to the arts (musical instruments, electronic organs, new paints, and sculpture materials)?

How has technology contributed to mathematics (computers, pocket calculators)?

How has technology contributed to science (new instruments in all fields, space research)?

How has technology contributed to good health?

How has technology contributed to military power? How has it changed power relationships among nations?

How can technology contribute to minimizing boring, repetitive jobs?

Are there any ghost towns in your area? Why were they abandoned? Was it due to a technological breakdown? An economic breakdown? Have technological breakdowns occurred in your town or city at certain times? Why did they occur?

What kinds of technological breakdowns may occur in the future? Do you think they are likely to get worse in time? What could be done to avoid them?

What effect does the introduction of modern technology have on nonindustrialized countries? Investigate this question for one country. Is the overall effect good or bad for the people of that country?

Consumer Education

Analyze commercials and advertisements (see chapter 10). Make up your own commercials to illustrate how they can mislead people. Why are people influenced by commercials?

Investigate food additives.

Investigate labeling for contents, calories, and medical effects.

Read labels and determine if they are adequate.

What effects do pesticides have on food and pollution?

What effect does packaging have on cost? On waste disposal? On air and water pollution?

What agencies protect the consumer? How effective are they?

How can consumers work together to protect themselves?

Investigate several recent consumer frauds.

Work out a program for better consumer protection.

Urban, Suburban, and Rural Life

Why did cities develop?

Investigate the history and manner of life in ancient cities that have disappeared, such as Babylon, Troy, or Uxmal.

What caused the decline of cities such as Venice, Genoa, or Santa Fe?

What are the advantages and disadvantages of cities to society? To individuals?

What are the advantages of rural living? The disadvantages?

In what ways do suburban life attempt to combine the advantages of both?

What role does plentiful energy play in the maintenance of modern cities? What would happen to such cities if energy became very scarce?

How has the automobile changed the relationship between city, country, and suburbia?

How could cities and farms be developed without destroying the natural environments of plants and animals?

Investigate population density and its effects on urban and rural areas.

How can buildings be constructed to minimize harmful effects on the environment?

What can be done to reduce the ugliness of some city and country areas?

How can crime be reduced?

How does the style of architecture of a city indicate its history?

Does your town or city use its land effectively? Could it be improved? It isn't easy to change the structure of a city once it is built. For example, compare the problems of constructing new bike paths after the streets are laid with building them as part of the original street plan.

Investigate the design and functioning of new planned cities such as Columbia, Maryland, or Reston, Virginia.

How are cities governed?

How do cities serve the social needs of the people (hospitals, schools, police, courts, etc.)? How would you improve the social services in your city or town?

How does a city affect the behavior and life styles of it's residents?

What is a neighborhood or community? How and why does it change with time? How does it affect the quality of life?

Design (in broad outline) what you consider to be an ideal community or city.

Inflation

What causes the current inflation? What is it worldwide?

Should the government take any steps to curb inflation or let it take its course? Why?

What should business do to curb inflation? What should labor do? What should consumers do?

Which economic groups are hit hardest by inflation? Which groups may benefit?

How does a worldwide shortage of energy (artificial or real) contribute to inflation?

Investigate the effect of each of the following factors on inflation: money supply, increasing demands for consumer goods, interest rates, business profits, labor contracts, government spending, government deficits, banking policies, Federal Reserve policies, gold and money speculators, and international politics.

What plans for curbing inflation seem most sound to you? Why?

World of Work[9]

What occupations would you consider for yourself? Why do you prefer them?

What are your personal goals in life? How can selection of an occupation further these goals?

Talk to people who work in the occupations you prefer. What do they consider the pros and cons of the job? What special skills are needed on these jobs?

What general types of occupations are there? (This question involves analyzing the relationships between different functions in the economy: production, marketing, servicing, distribution, research, development of new products, management, and labor.)

What are the pros and cons of civil service versus private industry?

---

[9] "Discovery," a career education program that focuses on personal values and goals, is available from Scholastic Book Services, Englewood Cliffs, N.J. 07632.

Develop a plan for preparing for an occupation you prefer.

Will college education help you reach your occupational goals? If so, what will it cost? How could you get supplementary funds? What colleges would you select to meet your needs?

Investigate one occupation in detail by talking to people who are working at it, by reading about it, and by visiting a place where the job is performed.

Economic conditions often change rapidly and leave trained people stranded without jobs. What are some occupations closely related to the one you selected which might offer alternatives?

In the specific career in which you are interested, is there any discrimination against minorities or women with respect to salary, working conditions, or promotion?

People in America

(Before investigating this topic the teacher should make clear that every individual has a worthy and interesting origin and need not be ashamed of it. Many poor people have more interesting backgrounds and experiences than rich people. Students whose parents or grandparents came to the United States as immigrants have a doubly interesting history in two lands. A discussion by the class of the need to be proud of one's origin is essential to avoid feelings of inferiority by some students.)

Trace your family history as far back as you can by obtaining information from parents and relatives. Make a family tree.

In what ways were the lives of your parents and grandparents different from yours? What special hardships did they have to endure? (A class visit and discussion by several elderly members of the community could be quite illuminating.)

Everybody in the United States has descended from someone who came from a foreign land, mainly within the past one hundred years. (Even the Indians are thought to have come from Asia some 11,000 years ago.) What were the countries of origin of your ancestors? Where did they live? Why did they come?

What is the origin or possible origin of your name?

Different customs often cause misunderstandings. Investigate some seemingly strange customs of other peoples. Do they make sense from their viewpoint? Do you practice some customs that may seem strange to them?

What is meant by a "stereotype?" Find examples of stereotypes in the everyday world, in conversations, in newspapers, and on radio or TV.

Some people generalize about entire groups of people as having certain undesirable characteristics. How do such generalizations affect patterns of discrimination against minorities?[10]

What discriminations against minorities remain to be remedied? What has been accomplished in recent times?

What part does economic status play in keeping minorities from achieving full equality?

What is an ethnic group?

Select an ethnic group for study. What contributions have members of the group made to society as a whole?

Why do ghettos develop?

War and Peace[11]

List the wars and police actions in which the United States has been involved.

Select a specific war for intensive study. What do historians think were the basic causes of that war? Did people of that time understand these basic causes, or did they go to war for other reasons? Did the war resolve the basic issues decisively? Did unresolved issues later produce wars?

Compare the basic conclusions for the war you studied with those for other wars investigated by other students.

Alfred Nobel thought his invention of violent explosives would make wars less likely. Was he correct and why?

---

[10] A unit, "Prejudice," part of the Contact series, is published by Scholastic Book Services, Englewood Cliffs, N.J. 07632.
[11] Information is available from the Center for War/Peace Studies, 218 East 18th St., New York, N.Y. 10003, and World Law Fund, 11 West 42nd St., New York, N.Y. 10036.

Some people say that nuclear bombs make wars between big powers less likely. Do you think they are right?

The Middle East wars of the recent past have been relatively brief, but the Vietnam war has dragged on for decades. What effect did terrain have on this difference? What other factors were involved?

Do you think it will ever be possible to eliminate all wars? How? Why?

Is man aggressive by nature? How have experts in different fields answered this question?

How do cultural differences, economic rivalries, racial antagonisms, nationalism, patriotism, and propaganda contribute to wars?

In what ways do nations interfere in the internal affairs of other nations?

Some people believe that peace in the modern world requires nations to give up some of their national sovereignty to international peace-making agencies. Is this desirable? Can it be achieved?

During every war some atrocities are committed on both sides. Why do officers and soldiers commit such atrocities despite official policies that forbid them? If you were a soldier and an officer ordered you to commit an illegal, immoral act, what would you do?

Why did the League of Nations fail as a peace-making agency?

How does the United Nations try to keep peace?

Human emotions aroused by war have been dramatically portrayed in a number of famous war novels, for example, *All Quiet on the Western Front* by Erich Maria Remarque, *Absent Without Leave* by Heinrich Böll, and *Farewell to Arms* by Ernest Hemingway. Read and compare these or other war novels with regard to their portrayal of the nature of war and what wars meant to the people who lived through them. Some of these novels have been made into movies which might be compared in a similar manner.

OTHER GENERAL TOPICS

Our Community
Education and the School
Human Resources
Natural Resources
Understanding Yourself
Understanding Other People
Understanding Parents
Understanding Brothers and
  Sisters
Architecture, Good and Bad
Industry, Pros and Cons
Improving the Distribution of
  Goods
How Local Government
  Functions
Politics in Your Town
Eliminating Political
  Corruption
The Prison System
The Death Penalty
Drug Abuse
Investigate an Industry or
  Business
Labor Unions
Improving Health Care
Fire Prevention
Improving Television
Newspapers, Good or Bad
Improving the Use of Radio
Land Use and Abuse
Air, a Precious Resource
Rivers, Lakes, and Oceans
Outer Space

How Books (or Newspapers)
  Are Written and Produced
Building a Home
Building a Bridge
What Is Good Art?
How Sculptors Work (make a
  piece of sculpture)
Painting a Picture
Music Today and Yesterday
A Finite Earth
Should Industry Keep
  Growing?
Controlling Population
What Is Life?
What Is the Real Purpose of
  Sex?
How Does Man Resemble All
  Other Mammals?
Man and Ape
Women's Liberation
Child Abuse
Rights and Responsibilities of
  Young People
Comparative Religions
What Is Time?
Gravity—Could We Do
  Without It?
Light—Suppose There Was
  None?
Problems of Old Age
Why Young and Old Disagree
City Planning
Mass Transportation

Improving Recreational Facilities

Cultural Differences

Nature of Conflict

The Human Mind

Mass Media

Justice and the Court System

Americans All

Consumer Law

Insurance Business—Should It Be More Strictly Regulated?

Body Language

Better Movies

Big Cars versus Small

Propaganda—How to Analyze It

Poverty, Its Cause and Cure

Causes of Dissent

Change, Today and Tomorrow

Maps

Liberty and Freedom

Problems of Democracy

Managing the Oceans

United Nations, Success or Failure?

World Law

Some Special Programs That Incorporate Reality-Centered Topics

SCIS (Science Curriculum Improvement Study) Physical and Life Science Programs, published by Rand McNally Co., Box 7600, Chicago, Ill. 60680. Fundamental concepts of change and interaction and organisms-environment interactions are used to develop physical science and life science units respectively. Basic physical scence concepts such as systems, models, and variables in life science concepts such as populations, environments, communities, and ecosystems have been utilized in social studies.

"New Science Courses Stress Solutions to Practical Problems," *New York Times*, Annual Education Review, January 16, 1974. This article describes the program, "Man-Made World," developed by Engineering Concepts Curriculum Project at the State University of New York at Stony Brook and similar programs elsewhere.

Nuffield Foundation Science Teaching Project, Chelsea College, University of London, Poulton Place, London S.W.6. Materials also published by Penguin Books, Inc., 7110 Ambassador Rd., Baltimore, Md. 21207.

Human Sciences: A Developmental Approach to Adolescent Education. Biological Sciences Curriculum Study, University of Colorado, Box 930, Boulder, Colo. 80302, 1973. This booklet projects a series of modules geared to the social, moral, and cognitive developmental levels of eleven- to thirteen-year-old students.

TETE (Total Education in the Total Environment) under the direction of William R. Eblen, Hudson River Museum, 511 Warburton Ave., Yonkers, N.Y. 10701, 1971. This experimental program, funded by the New York State Council of the Arts, represents a multidisciplinary approach aiming "to demonstrate the relationship between ecological studies, social values, and personal attitudes and ethics in order to reexamine the place and role of man in his total environment." The program has developed an Ecology Series published by Pendulum Press, Academic Bldg., Saw Mill Rd., West Haven, Conn. 06510.

"Crisis in America," *Social Education*, November 1973, vol. 37, no. 7. This article describes a high school social studies course designed by teachers using students' suggestions and questions related to: environmental problems, crisis in education, technology, race relations, housing. Students helped develop reading lists, consulted community resource people, and organized and taught a short series of lessons to others in the class. The teacher was the facilitator, helping to identify and clarify problems and assisting students in maintaining a multidisciplinary focus.

Miniguides: 16 Ready-Made Mini-Courses, prepared by the editors of *Scholastic Teacher*, Citation Press, New York, N.Y. 10036, 1975. Activities and multimedia resources for short courses on sexual identity, the supernatural, peace and war, folklore, mysteries, violence, death, loneliness and alienation, biography, humor, survival, energy, American labor, art of criticism, science fiction, and living with handicaps.

TECHNIQUES FOR GENERATING REALITY-CENTERED ACTIVITIES

✺ Reality-centered topics, courses, or minicourses that focus on major problems of our time are readily suggested by the headlines in the daily newspapers, but the potential is much broader than that. The fact is that reality-centered units may be generated from *any* aspect of the real environment. All one need do is to look around—in the classroom, in the streets, at home, in the woods, up in the sky, in a pond or lake, or in the halls of Congress or the state legislature. There are real social, political, economic, psychological, and language elements in *any* feature of the environment, and reality-minded teachers can readily relate the real world to abstract principles to any extent they desire. They can also approach any aspect of the real world from the viewpoint of the particular subject they are licensed to teach, preferably integrating it with other subject areas.

AN ILLUSTRATION: ANALYZING WORDS IN A BOOK

Normally studying a book would be considered the province of English teachers; they would be expected to treat a book as a piece of literature or use it for reading practice. But it is also possible to study a book from other viewpoints. For example, many kinds of questions may be asked about the letters, words, sentences, paragraphs, and chapters—and answers may be obtained by individual investigation. "Which is the longest word?" "The shortest?" "Which word is repeated the most?" "Which letter is used the most?" "Are there more consonants than vowels?"

In upper level English classes integrative-minded teachers might suggest analyzing the style differences of two authors. "What types of words are used?" "Are the words and sentences long or short?" "Are many adjectives used or few?" "What proportion of the copy is dialogue?" "Are paragraphs long or short?" They could suggest that students devise a set of characteristics with which one could distinguish each author. The students could then test their hypotheses with actual experiments. The purpose would be to examine elements of style and to encourage students to observe carefully how outstanding authors choose and use words.

In a mathematics or science class, an investigation of letters and words in a book could delve deeply into probability and statistics. Everyone in the class might be asked to select any page of any book and count a given number of consecutive letters—at least 200, but preferably 500. Each then prepares a list of each letter ranked by frequency of occurrence. Students will be astonished to find that their lists of most frequently occurring letters are almost identical.

All the data may be combined, and percentages of occurrence may be calculated by computation or with a calculator or slide rule. This establishes an excellent sample set of data that may be compared with more extensive studies reported in some encyclopedias. Students will find that *e* occurs close to 13 percent of the time, t close to 10 percent, while x, j and z will be less than one-half percent.

Although the mathematics required is of a simple type that most seventh graders can do, students have a real experience with the kind of statistical data-gathering that is undertaken in most research projects and in the everyday business world. They will obtain a feeling for the predictive value of statistics in an investigation, whether it be as a medical researcher, anthropologist, economist, or businessman.

There are many ways of applying the information. For example, if a rather long cryptogram (200 letters or more) is composed without using artificial or difficult language, it is generally very easy to identify the main letters solely by comparing frequencies of occurrence. Some students will be interested in composing and solving cryptograms. Others may investigate other statistical data about words and letter combinations. "What are the most frequently used two-letter words?" "Three-letter words?" "What letters are most frequently found in two-letter words?" "Three-letter words?" "Do letters appear in preferential positions in words?" "What letters are frequently found as final letters?" "Initial letters?"

Activities can involve counting, recognizing, observing, gathering data, recording data, exercising initiative, thinking, reasoning, communicating, explaining, working with others, all experiences that develop concepts and are based on something real and immediate. The study begins at an essentially concrete, sensory level but rapidly moves into abstract areas easily controlled by the teacher or students who initiate their own activities.

ACTIVITIES FROM THE ENVIRONMENT

Normally most subjects are taught in a highly structured sequence of lessons based on a logically developed conceptual scheme. This pattern produces very formalized learnings, which tend to crowd out the creative aspects of learning in which questions are devised and answers searched for. To include these essential investigations, teachers should allot some time to exploring elements of the environment. Anything in the real world—an event, phenomenon, object, material, plant or animal, person or group—can be the subject of investigation at any level from kindergarten to college and beyond. Success will depend on the abilities of the investigator, not the nature of the subject.

Water in a clear plastic tumbler might be investigated in detail in a science class. The teacher might suggest that students try to find out all they can about the water. One may observe that his finger appears magnified when placed in the tumbler, another notices that a pencil placed in the water appears broken, and still another sees mirror reflections. These observations could lead to investigations of refraction of light, lenses, and mirrors. Another student may observe that her finger becomes wet when dipped into water. Most objects are moistened by water, but oily surfaces and some plastics are not. These facts have an important bearing on molecular forces, which are studied at higher levels.

The observation that a sugar cube dissolves in water may lead to investigations of the solubility of various substances. More sugar dissolves in a glass of water, for instance, than salt. Another student may discover that a blue dye and a yellow dye produce a green color when mixed. This may lead to an investigation of the principles of mixing colors with paints, crayons, and transparent plastics. This activity has important applications to art as well as to science.

A student may drop a paper clip into a glass full to the brim and observe that the water does not spill over. This suggests the question, "How many clips can you add to the water before it begins to spill?" Students will observe that the water rising higher and higher above the rim of the glass, without spilling, forms a convex surface, an observation that could lead to an investigation of surface tension.

Drops of water are fascinating to study. They can form on pencil tips, plastic covers of dishes, window panes, or a faucet.

They have interesting shapes and sizes on different materials. A drop of water on wax paper placed on a newspaper becomes a magnifier and enlarges the letters on the newsprint.

Answering the question, "How many drops are in a glass of water?" involves basic concepts such as counting, sampling, and estimating. Instead of directly counting actual drops in a glass, students might do the following. First the number of drops in a small vial are counted directly, then the number of vials full of water required to fill the glass are counted. Simple multiplcation gives the total number of drops. Many students will, by themselves, work out the indirect but time-saving process of sampling to arrive at an estimate.

"Is a drop of oil larger or smaller than one of water?" The answer is obtained by observing how many drops of each substance fill a small vial. The relative sizes (volumes) of the drops of oil and water may be estimated from the ratio of the number of drops for each. "What does a drop of water or of oil weigh?" The answer is obtained by weighing a large number of counted drops and dividing the results.

There seems to be no limit to the creative activities that can be generated for a science class around the subject of water—floating, sinking, boiling, freezing, dissolving, evaporating, flowing, bubbling, properties of light, volume, counting, estimating, sampling, weighing, shapes of surfaces, expansion and contraction, temperature, heating effects, use in batteries, importance to plants, raining, snowing, and so on.

Although most of the phenomena associated with a tumblerful of water would be considered science with some mathematical content, there is really no reason to limit them. Reading and writing can be initiated on the subject of water. Poetry about seas, rivers, or lakes, or ocean life, boating, or fishing may be written or read. Imaginative songs may be composed and sung. Art may be introduced by observing, drawing, or photographing the beautiful and varied hexagonal structures of snow crystals or the curved, rainbow-colored light patterns created by sunlight passing through a goblet of water. Since man's life everywhere depends to a great extent on the availability of water, investigations may be related to history, politics, economics, and technology.

The point is that water can serve as the mainspring for a wide variety of reality-centered studies. The same can be said of air, earth, space, mountains, deserts, factories, people, animals, and any other object, material, or event. The source of subjects for study is essentially limitless. Actual choice of a subject may be based on a balanced combination of what students are most interested in and what society feels they need to know.

GENERATING INVESTIGATIONS

Once a subject is selected, questions about it must be generated. Sometimes questions are obvious and are suggested by the nature of the event or thing, but more often a brainstorming session is helpful to raise questions that can serve as springboards for investigation. One technique for generating questions is a game of ten questions. A student is called upon to name a noun, i.e., captain, gun, horse, senator, or ink, or a verb, i.e., wait, ride, dig, drop, die, or complain. Each sudent in the class is then asked to think of ten meaningful questions about the word that would be suitable for investigation. Two teams can also offer questions alternately. When one team can no longer think of any questions, the other team wins.

Although some students will find it difficult to think of ten questions at first, collectively they will produce a large number which, when read to the class, will stimulate less imaginative students to produce meaningful questions on their own. For example, here are some typical questions that might be asked about the verb "sit": Can anyone sit perfectly still? How long can one sit still? Why do people have different sitting positions? How does the design of a chair assist people to sit? Why do people spend so much time sitting? What are some different sitting customs in different cultures? How do different animals sit? Why can't fish sit? How can one tell if a person or animal is sitting? How many different meanings does the word "sit" have?

Although all these questions are potentially of interest and value, one would be hard put to find ready answers to any of them in books in the average library. One wonders if some of these questions have ever been investigated at all. Students will begin to see that possible creative investigations are almost limitless if they can devise interesting questions.

Once a meaningful question or problem has been selected, a number of basic techniques should be brought into play, depending upon the level of the students. These techniques can be developed to maximum effectiveness by repeated use at ever-increasing levels of sophistication throughout the years.

One of the simplest investigational tools for younger children is observation in the broad sense of using any or all of one's senses, not just sight. For example, if the question being investigated is, "Does each person have different sitting positions?" the children would simply watch people sitting and describe their positions. Such observations could be done by a kindergarten child or by an engineer working on an analysis of sitting positions for a chair manufacturer. Various instruments could aid the observations. At a simple level one could take photographs to make a permanent record, or at a more sophisticated level one could take various measurements to determine the degrees of slouch.

At the simplest levels observations do not require that one do anything other than watch or listen or feel. Observers do not tamper with their subjects or interact with them, but if they do begin to modify a situation by moving things around or setting up or arranging special circumstances, then they introduce an element of experimentation. Thus, a wooden chair may be offered to a subject and observations made about how he sits in it; then the subject may be offered a soft chair and similar observations made. A number of people may be observed sitting in these and other kinds of chairs. The experimental procedures may become so complex that it may become necessary to use special observing instruments (microscopes, telescopes, magnifiers, amplifiers) or measuring instruments to obtaining data. A place to house and use them, a laboratory, may be required. But the ultimate purpose of all these trappings is to generate observations that are applicable to the problem to which a solution is sought.

Various mathematical techniques may be applied to the data. At the lowest levels this may consist merely of counting—numbers of items, or people, or positions, or minutes, seconds, inches, and so on. At higher levels calculations are made with the data, perhaps with a calculator or computer. Possible relationships and hypotheses will be thought of. Then the hypotheses will be tested, and eventually certain conclusions will be reached, which are essentially the answers to the original question and perhaps to others that have arisen during the investigation.

Various resources may be required for investigating what others have learned concerning the matters under study. At the younger levels information will be obtained mainly from others—from peers, parents, teachers, or other adults. At a more advanced level the investigation may utilize printed information in books and in libraries. There may be conferences with peers or colleagues to exchange information, especially when investigations are performed by a group in which each individual undertakes a different phase of the study.

Experience with these techniques may be built into any investigation at any level of development.

GIVING REALITY TO ABSTRACT SUBJECTS

Suppose that the legislative process is being studied in a social studies class, and the teacher desires to introduce some reality content into the learnings. Students could be asked to brainstorm some questions about legislatures. One question might be, "What does a Congressman do?" If students decide to investigate the question, they could go to a library to look up a Congressman's voting record in the *Congressional Record* or write letters asking for information about his or her positions on various issues. Each response by the Congressman on an issue could lead to its own side investigation. A personal visit might be arranged at his home office or his staff might be interviewed. An experiment might be set up to assess voter knowledge or opinions of the Congressman's work.

The investigation could well lead to a public report about the Congressman and perhaps a class evaluation of his record, pro and con. If an election is pending, individual members of the class could be stimulated to work in his behalf or for an opponent, thereby bringing the reality process to its logical conclusion and giving students a fruitful experience in citizenship that would be far more meaningful than any class-confined activity.

Could such a reality approach be applied to the highly abstract subject of mathematics? Actually, it is possible to develop most mathematical concepts within a reality framework by working from a real-life situation toward a concept. As an example, assume that a teacher in an algebra class conducts a lesson on the class of equations for the form $y = ax^2$ (x^2 means x multiplied by itself). The customary equation for a falling body, $d = 16t^2$, belongs to this class of mathematical equations. The study of this equation could be illustrated as follows. Students are asked to work in pairs to perform the following activity. One student holds a ruler at the twelve-inch mark, between his thumb and forefinger, so that it hangs down vertically. The partner places his thumb and forefinger at the beginning of the ruler (zero position) so that his fingers almost touch it. The first student drops the ruler; the second grasps it as quickly as he can as it falls.

After a few trials most people grasp the ruler at the six-inch mark, more or less. There is a certain lag—known as reaction time—because of the operation of the nervous system. One sees the ruler released, an impulse goes from the eyes to the brain, mulls around for an instant, and triggers a command to the fingers to grasp the ruler; one then grasps it, but by that time, it has fallen a certain distance.

"Can the distance the ruler falls be used to estimate reaction time?" Galileo showed that the distance an object falls in a given time is expressed in the formula $d = 16t^2$, where d is distance in feet and t is time in seconds. For distances measured in inches, the formula would be modified as follows:

$$d = 16t^2 \text{ (in feet)}$$
$$= 12 \times 16t^2 \text{ (in inches)}$$
$$= 192t^2 \text{ (in inches)}$$

To encourage initiative, suggest that students try to figure out for themselves, overnight or over a weekend, how to use this information to calculate reaction time from the measured distance fallen by the ruler. Even if only a handful succeed, this is one way to provide for the needs of the mathematically inclined students.

A simple method is to calculate the distance the ruler would fall for brief, but increasingly greater times until the theoretical distance of fall matches the actual distance fallen. Students could construct a table of distances versus time, as follows:

t (seconds)	d (inches)
.10	1.92
.11	2.32
.12	2.76
.13	3.24
.14	3.76
.15	4.32
.16	4.92
.17	5.55
.18	6.22
.19	6.93
.20	7.68

It is readily apparent from the table that the time the ruler takes to fall six inches is close to .18 second. It may, therefore, be inferred that the reaction time is .18 second or less, since some slight time is required for the fingers to move.

In this activity a simple ruler is used to accurately estimate reaction time to within one-hundredth of a second! (It is possible to differentiate between 0.18 second and 0.17 or 0.19). This achievement relates science to mathematics and illustrates the important techniques of indirect measurement so vital to discovering properties of difficult-to-observe phenomena. Students also receive a dramatic demonstration justifying the judgment of some scholars that mathematics is the "queen of sciences," and they may obtain a healthier respect for the usefulness of mathematical knowledge.

There are many similar real life circumstances around which the mathematics curriculum can be designed to make students feel that this traditionally abstract subject is of importance to them. Concepts in trigonometry, such as the meaning and use of sine, cosine, and tangent, could be developed in the context of a real problem, perhaps measuring the distance across a nearby river. Architectural shapes in the community—domes, arches, triangular roofs, trusses, or bridges—could provide real-life motivation to study geometry, both two dimensional and solid.

Study of a real camera could introduce the problems of properly setting the lens opening and shutter time for best exposure, and this in turn could lead students to study their mathematical relationships (concepts involving the area of a circle, inverse square relationships between shutter time and diameter of the lens opening) and if they desire to pursue the matter, the relationships of reciprocals in the lens distance formula.

FILMS AND TELEVISION

Young people spend such a large amount of time watching television and movies that it is common sense to use them as major resources for generating reality-centered activities. Use of these resources by alert teachers is fine, but better yet are programs (not yet widespread) in which school systems utilize existing TV programs and movies for educational purposes.

One such effort has been undertaken in an experimental program in Philadelphia based in fifteen schools.[1] Reading lessons were based on the scripts for popular TV programs, such as "Sanford and Son," "Kung Fu," and "The FBI." The telecast shows were videotaped at an audiovisual center and then presented in classes. Verbatim scripts obtained from the producers were mimeographed and given to students in grades five through eight for lessons in reading and writing. Familiarity and reality made these reading and writing experiences far more motivating than traditional readers. Teachers reported that students at the lower levels of achievement "turned on" to these scripts and rapidly improved their reading skills. Also fewer cut class, attention was much more intense, and discipline problems tended to disappear. A major factor in the increased interest and achievement was the wholesale application of the concrete sensory elements of sight and sound to reading. Students followed the scripts as they watched the action and heard the words spoken "for real" by professional actors. The abstract words on the printed page came alive.

The role of the administration in planning and organizing is critical for the success of such a program. The main point of the program would be lost if the taped shows could not be presented in class for students to watch as they read the scripts. The administration not only supplies the tapes, duplicated scripts, and classroom TV sets but also organizes the distribution of materials and provides training for the teachers. This is the type of reality-centered program that could not be successful without intensive effort at all levels. TV is a complex tool and will prove costly and useless in the classroom unless there is intelligent planning, coupled with adequate budget and competent staff.

The activities emanating from the program, although intended mainly to teach reading, have many other divergent outcomes. Students become interested in acting out the roles, and they have

---

[1] Additional information about the program may be obtained from Dr. Michael Marcase, Associate Superintendent, Philadelphia Public Schools.

the scripts to make this possible, plus actual examples to imitate. Formerly reluctant students become stimulated to read aloud, and correctly. They may discover that the humorous lines they read aloud often do not seem funny at all but are when professional actors speak the lines. "Why?" Striving to produce real humor helps students begin to master the difficult art of acting. These activities have important psychological pluses, particularly for students normally reluctant to participate in class, and they have considerable potential for improving self-image.

Some schools already have videotape cameras that can be operated by students, offering real-life experiences in writing, acting, managing, and producing local shows. At a higher level is the type of program produced by WRC-TV in Washington, D.C., in which young people from eleven to fifteen years of age serve as reporters for the "Youth News" show that appears on prime time. Such programs could be integrated into the classroom with videotape or videocassettes.

And don't overlook the standard shows such as "Sesame Street" and "The Electric Company," which feature reality-centered content mainly for individual passive watching by children. These programs will always have a function, both inside the classroom and out, but they merely scratch the surface of the potential for generating reality-centered activities.

USING MUSIC

Even superficial observation of the world of teenagers quickly reveals that popular songs play an important part in the lives of most of them. Whenever teachers observe such a vital aspect of their students' lives, it should ring a bell in their heads—"Aha! Here is something that could generate reality-centered activities."

Songs can motivate learning in a wide range of areas. In English classes, and to a lesser extent in social studies classes, popular songs can provide material for discussion and writing, particularly material related to understanding emotions and feelings.[2] Some possibilities are suggested in the following brief quotations from a number of popular songs and folk songs:

> Welcome, sulphur dioxide./ Hello, carbon monoxide./ The air, the air is ev'rywhere./ Breathe deep while you sleep; breathe deep. ("Air" by James Rado and Gerome Ragni)[3]

> He is trampling on the vineyard/ Where the grapes of wrath are stored ("The Battle Hymn of the Republic" by Julia Ward Howe and William Steffe)

> No more auction block for me—no more, no more. ("No More Auction Block," Negro spiritual)

Naturally, a record or tape of the entire song should be played several times so that students are able to assess the full meaning of the emotions and content. Once this has been done for several songs, students will begin to listen more carefully to the words (as will you) and will begin to suggest other songs that might be used for classroom purposes.

As is often the case, students can provide information and perceptive evaluations about the less publicized leaders of the popular music scene. The following comments illustrate students' feelings about themselves when reacting to popular songs as well their thoughts about artists as prophets and current social issues:

> Carly Simon touches you at the heart.

> Some song people are writers, generalists, and even poets, like Carole King.

> Just like in classical music, Emerson, Lake and Palmer don't emphasize words.

---

[2] E. L. Cooper. "Social Change, Popular Music and the Teacher," *Social Education*, December 1973.

[3] © 1966, 1967, 1968 James Rado, Gerome Ragni, Galt McDermont, Nat Shapiro, and United Artists Music Co., Inc. All rights administered by United Artists Music Co., Inc., New York, NY 10019. Used by permission.

The garish and ghoulish dress and images displayed by Alice Cooper shows that he is spitting in the face of the Establishment; he's rebelling.

I appreciate David Bowie for his fantasy-rich words and his feelings of space.

People who follow the Mahavishnu Orchestra show how they dig oriental religious motifs and the acid rock of electric guitars.

It is even possible to introduce academic concepts with songs. Here, for example, is a song (with a very catchy tune sung by Tom Glazer) used in grades six through nine to introduce the concept, "Work equals force times distance." Usually this concept is taught in physics courses in the eleventh or twelfth grades.

How Do We Measure Energy

How do we measure Energy? . . . in foot pounds . . . foot pounds
How do we know it gets to be . . . a foot pound . . . foot pound
The energy expended by . . . lifting one pound one foot high
That's one . . . foot pound . . . that's one . . . foot pound
The foot pound measures Energy! . . .

Pick up an object from the ground . . . Easy . . . does it
Say that the object weighs ten pounds . . . ten pounds . . . ten pounds
Lift up the object four feet high, ten by four you multiply
That's forty . . . foot pounds . . . forty . . . foot pounds
The foot pound measures Energy!
The foot pound measures Energy![4]

---

[4] Lyric by Hy Zaret Music by Lou Singer   from Energy & Motion Songs (Ballads For The Age Of Science) copyright 1961 by Argosy Music Corporation.

After listening to the record, a number of questions can be asked: "What is meant by energy?" "What is a foot pound?" "What is the purpose of measuring foot pounds?" "Which takes more energy, lifting 10 pounds 20 feet, or 3 pounds 75 feet?" Questions like these can extend the concepts in a way students will enjoy, because they were introduced with a sensory experience. This reality technique is particularly useful in nonacademic classes where it is desirable to reduce the abstract content of traditional lessons.

MOTIVATION
IN THE LIGHT
OF REALITY

§ In an educational context, motivation is simply the desire to learn. Without the desire, little or no learning occurs in school situations. Chapter 2, Educational Realities, dealt with general principles of young people's development and discussed general factors that contribute to interest or disinterest. This chapter focuses on specific techniques for motivating students.

Failure to motivate students to learn is a major cause of ineffective education. On the other hand, appropriate motivation, often generated by teachers, opens the door to learning, expels fears, liberates students' resources, and generally sets the stage for productive learning. Strongly motivated students will make every effort to learn, while unmotivated students couldn't care less.

What motivates students and makes them want to learn? As with most questions in education, the answer is highly individual and varies with each student and each situation. Nevertheless, there are general guidelines that can help teachers to encourage students to want to learn.

Society itself motivates people to perform certain kinds of acts that it considers desirable and not to do what it considers undesirable. One simple type of motivation is the fear of punishment. In the schools this may consist of threats—to keep students after school or to call up parents—or actual punishment may be meted out—poor marks, detention, or tongue lashings. Threats, fears, and punishments can force some young people to pay attention to their lessons. Since fear is a motivating force in the real world, at least students learn what the real world is like, but fear-based motivation can have some unpleasant results.

In contrast, motivation by some kind of reward, either material or psychological, is superior for educational purposes. In the real world, human beings have a wide range of motivations, including rewards, privileges, and money. People are strongly influenced by the approval and disapproval of others and by personal recognition for their efforts. In the classroom praise must be given judiciously and matched to the needs of the learner. Frequent praise for small accomplishments may be essential for a student who has failed at everything and is starved for recognition, but it tends to become hollow when overused with students who resent being spoon-fed or who become overdependent and will not perform if not praised.

The opinions of one's peers are very effective motivators, but society may not always agree with what the peer group thinks is appropriate in terms of dress or group behavior. It is unfortunate that schools have not developed methods of utilizing peer pressures for more positive ends. Some community youth workers have shown how it can be done in the real world of the streets, and their methods could probably be adapted to schools.

Many students do have a desire to learn but, as teachers know, too many others do not. Basic motivation to learn is fostered by favorable factors at home—loving parents who encourage achievement at school, serve as models of behavior, and provide the kinds of activities that prepare children for success in school. Schools can build on the motivation provided at home if they provide an education students enjoy and see as worthwhile. An effective program of reality-centered education certainly strengthens motivation, which is stimulated by reality-centered activities and fostered by school environments that are pleasant and reasonably orderly, by teachers who are encouraged to do their best, and by supervisors who know their business and perform effectively.

In the classroom teachers can contribute to basic motivation by finding out as much as they can about their students as individuals —what turns them on and what their interests are outside of school.

PERSONAL SUCCESS TECHNIQUES

In the real world a major motivation to work as well as to learn new tasks is the satisfaction derived from the activities. One student may relish a good mathematical puzzle; another will eagerly participate in a dramatic performance; still another jumps at the chance to construct something.

Studies of the work of creative scientists indicate that many are motivated more by problem-solving factors than by a potential for usefulness. There seems to be a basic human curiosity or need-to-know that motivates investigation and, incidentally, learning. We see this type of motivation in young people who want to solve puzzles, ranging from simple jigsaw puzzles for young children to mathematical puzzles at higher levels.

Closely related are game and play activities that seem to be enjoyable in and of themselves, providing another possible motivational route in the classroom.

Displaying drawings, paintings, sculptures, or constructions serves as a strong motivator for creativity. Nothing will stimulate students to create art than to hold their work up for approval, put it on a bulletin board, or display it in a hall cabinet with their names on it.

Some teachers use a technique in which they humorously bestow real-world titles for work well done. An outstanding job could rate the designation of President, while a good job might earn the title of Governor, Senator, or Mayor. Rewards for achievement, which have the effect of stimulating additional accomplishment, can take many forms depending largely on the ingenuity of the teacher, ranging from the granting of special privileges for work well done (leading a group, taking part in a play) to special activities (attending special events or trips).

The more fundamental and more desirable motivation is to succeed in mastering one's schoolwork. Most children enter school with the hope and expectation that they will learn to read, calculate, understand, and "grow up." They have a basic desire to fit into the real society they know and to become members in good standing. The immediate pressure for approval by parents, family, and peers plays a large role in these expectations. If children meet these expectations by learning what they are taught in school, then they receive family and societal approval, and the sweet smell of success further stimulates them to do the work they are asked to do, whether or not the teacher gives gold stars or offers special goodies and dispensations. Earning high marks to win parental and teacher approval is a complementary stimulus. For such children success becomes a way of life. They expect to succeed in learning and so does everybody else, and this drives them to further effort that generally leads to continued success.

The situation is quite the opposite for children who begin with failure or later stumble and fail. Such failure is often traumatic because of the adverse effects that inevitably follow—parent and teacher disapproval, punishments, and perhaps even by withdrawal of love. These disastrous consequences often spill over into relationships with one's peers, and a student may become the dummy, the butt of jokes, or the last one in the pecking order. Eventually, children who fail anticipate failure before it happens and are self-fulfillingly driven to reduce their learning efforts.

In many schools today one may observe extreme cases of

failure—nonreading teenagers who cut classes, hang around the toilets, engage in horseplay, or sit sullenly or resignedly until the time in "prison" is up. To most teachers such students appear totally unmotivated, and this may be true in English, or algebra, or history classes, which have no point for them as long as they are constantly reminded how stupid they are. But nonreaders may be highly intelligent individuals in matters that interest them outside of school. Some teachers who have carefully observed such students find that some have developed considerable skill in calculating probabilities and percentages in games using cards or dice or baseball and football, all of which they are motivated to learn.

Nonreaders generally have a strong underlying motivation to learn to read. First and foremost, they long to regain self-respect by proving to themselves and to the world that they are really not as dumb as others think and that they could learn if they had the chance. On the other hand, from bitter experience they come to believe that they are too stupid to learn. Secondly, as they approach adulthood they become increasingly aware of what a terrible handicap it is to be unable to read and to be so ignorant in an area where many seven-year-olds are competent. They also know they can never obtain a license to drive a car, an affront to their sense of adultness. And they have begun to observe that most good jobs are out of reach because of their illiteracy. They may even find it difficult to take a bus ride to a new place because they can't read the names of the streets and are too ashamed to ask others for help.

The reality for such "hopeless cases" is that learning to read would be an achievement representing a major turning point in life—one which, if students thought it possible, could provide very powerful motivation for learning. When schools actively seek out these boys and girls and approach them individually with appropriate efforts to teach them to read, they generally respond with rekindled hope and determination to learn. With the first success in learning to read, most nonreaders respond affirmatively, moti-ation to learn is restored and generally hostility toward school is substantially reduced.

Taking time to point out the future usefulness or practical applications of subject content can provide strong motivation to learn. As an illustration, the following technique was used with sixteen-year-old boys with very low achievement levels in an applied physics class. On the first day the discussion began, not with the subject of physics but with the question, "What kind of job would you like to have when you get out of school?" After a brief exchange the teacher asked, "How about a job as a fireman?" The response was quite favorable. To the boys in this class a job as a fireman seemed the height of achievable ambition. Doctor, teacher, or lawyer all represented pie-in-the-sky professions, the mention of which generally evoked sardonic laughter, but nobody in the class laughed at the idea of being a fireman.

"How do you get a job as fireman?" They knew about the physical requirements—running, jumping, climbing, and general fitness. Some had also heard about a written test. "Would you like to see a fireman's test?" They certainly did want to see one.

Copies of an old firemen's test, obtained from the New York City Civil Service Commission, were then distributed. The boys were suddenly absorbed—and astounded—in a confrontational situation with a high degree of reality for them. Here were hard-to-read questions that involved knowledge of mathematics, chemistry, current events, and the ability to reason from a verbal problem. One question (paraphrased) involved calculation of area: "A restaurant measures 60 feet by 100 feet. If the minimum allowable floor area per person is 12 square feet, what is the maximum number of persons allowed in the restaurant?"

The boys would not stop until every one of the sixty test questions had been thoroughly discussed and answered, a task that occupied several periods. They also had an opportunity to examine copies of exams for jobs as policeman, mason's helper (with many problems about suitable quantities for mixing cement), plumber's helper, station attendant, and the like. All this did not seem to be directly applicable to applied physics, but after that job motivation unit, the teacher had no problem justifying a reading assignment or written responses to questions. Suddenly the boys became interested in spelling and writing.

In view of the importance of this type of long-range motivation, curriculum makers should design appropriate units in each subject area, with accompanying materials, to indicate how the subject might help a student prepare for a career in the adult world. This kind of motivation is especially effective with students who are not interested in their studies, especially if they can see that what they learn could help them get a better job.

QUESTIONS, CURIOSITY, AND PHYSICAL ACTIVITIES

Every good teacher strives to elicit questions from students, usually within the framework and content of a single lesson. Rarely do teachers utilize the motivational potential of student questions for an entire unit or topic because they are then obligated to consider these questions to the satisfaction of the students, probably at the expense of the specific content of the preplanned sequence of lessons. But what happens if a teacher solicits questions about a topic or unit before its content is locked into final form? Students will raise questions that would normally not be considered by the teacher, but they are their questions, not the teacher's, and are therefore of greater natural interest. Motivation for learning is thereby enhanced.

For example, a teacher of a health unit in grades six to eight found to his surprise that when students in a number of classes were asked what they were interested in studying, about one-third wanted to learn about heart attacks and circulatory problems. Probably this reflected experiences with such ailments within the family, or maybe it reflected TV viewing with its numerous episodes involving death by heart attack. The existing curriculum allotted very little time for this topic, probably on the theory that it was more important to teach young people about good diet and brushing teeth than to be concerned about diseases of middle and old age.

Of course, it is desirable for teachers to alter the content of units to conform with what interests significant numbers of students. That would be a truly reality-oriented approach. It would be wise for subject departments to regularly survey student interests and teachers' suggestions to help revise or update units of study. Content is sometimes locked into a predetermined sequence with department examinations based on the same content for all classes. In such cases it would be best for the department to alter the content of courses to conform with student interests, as indicated by their questions, or else for teachers to be allowed flexibility to adapt units to the felt needs of their students.

Another effective type of motivation is activities in which students *do* something that is different in nature and quality from traditional discussion. Motion involving kinesthetic and sensory experiences make learning concrete instead of abstract and thus more interesting. The field trip is one common type of activity of this kind that is especially useful if it effectively introduces a topic. A high school biology teacher could organize a study of a local pond or assign a square yard of earth to each student to investigate the living things it contains. A mathematics teacher might arrange for a trip to a computer operation at a local business office.

A more extended project might be undertaken to stimulate interest by doing. For example, a history class of Dave Curran, a teacher in Corvallis, Oregon, built a twenty-foot flatboat of the type once used to carry cargo on the Mississippi and Ohio Rivers. Materials were donated by the community. No doubt, Mr. Curran's future classes will be motivated to study about life in early America by taking a ride on that flatboat.

"Doing" types of motivation need not be so extensive; they can be undertaken right in the classroom at a simpler level. A history teacher might obtain old maps of a region under study and compare them with recent maps. A mathematics teacher about to begin a unit on trigonometric functions could have students measure the distances from their desks to the nearest wall of the room, using protractors and graphical methods. At a later time he could demonstrate how sines, cosines, and tangents can do the job with greater accuracy and much less physical difficulty. Such activities bring feelings of reality and immediacy to a lesson. Lessons based on experience shift toward the concrete, away from the abstract, and become more meaningful to students.

Often a motivational doing activity may not seem directly related to the concepts or skills the teacher wishes to develop but actually encompasses them in a real-life manner. For example, a teacher working with difficult and slow boys and girls who were poor readers or nonreaders suggested that they take him on a neighborhood walk and point out interesting scenes to include in a large map-mural. This activity caught their interest, and they returned to the selected places to photograph them. Names of streets had to be read and written down. Directions for getting to the places were prepared. A small map was made from which the larger map-mural would be produced, involving map-making skills as well as reading and writing. During class discussions students were asked to comment on each photograph; they took particular pride in showing themselves and their friends in the pictures. All in all, a wide range of concepts and skills in reading, writing, oral presentation, mathematics, and art were touched upon, all within a learning-by-doing framework that built up feelings of satisfaction and self-worth.

Many higher mammals have been observed to possess a curiosity that impels them to investigate unusual objects and events they encounter. Man has this quality to an unusual degree. Many recreation and leisure activities are of a curiosity-arousing and satisfying nature—the mystery story, the whodunit movie, why-does-it-happen books, TV documentaries, and daily news reports. "What is happening?" "How does it happen?" "Why does it happen?" "Where will it lead?" "Why is the world the way it is?"

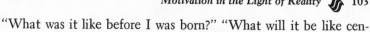

"What was it like before I was born?" "What will it be like centuries from now?" Such questions about the world are of deep interest to most individuals and especially to young people in their formative years. Lessons that begin with curiosity-arousing experiences effectively motivate students to think about the study at hand, especially if they relate to questions at an appropriate level.

CONFRONTATION AND CHALLENGE TECHNIQUES

Puzzles and games are excellent motivational devices because they challenge students and dare them to use their minds. There is a strong element of ego-satisfaction in puzzle and game activities because youngsters can prove their ability to perform difficult mental feats. A puzzle or game should be presented in a setting that does not directly pit one student against another personally or psychologically. Many students react with anxiety to the risk of losing in a strongly competitive situation, and this may destroy the motivation the teacher planned.

Any confrontation in the realm of ideas includes an element of reality because students feel impelled to resolve the challenge to their sense of right and wrong, their moral values, or their sense of logic. The problem is to design activities for each topic that will provide a suitable confrontation or will arouse students' desires to satisfy their curiosity. Remember that the motivational technique is not an end in itself but is merely a vehicle for achieving more effective learning. Sometimes teachers are so carried away by the motivational technique that it becomes the tail that wags the educational dog.

Recently a teacher met a former student who vividly recalled the motivation for the generally run-of-the-mill subject of the mechanical advantage of a wheel and axle. The lesson had begun routinely with a humdrum review of the concepts developed the previous day. But before beginning the review, the teacher asked a student to fill a glass of water in preparation for an experiment. He dutifully went up to the front of the room to fetch the water, while the teacher proceeded with the review. Soon all eyes wandered to watch the student, ignoring the teacher. Obviously the student was having some difficulty obtaining his glass of water. The reason? Before the lesson, the faucet handle had been removed, and the student was confronted with only the shaft jutting out of the water pipe and nothing with which to grip it.

"What's the trouble?" the teacher asked.

"I can't get any water. The handle is missing."

"Well, the shaft is sticking out. Can't you turn that?"

The student dutifully tried again, but the shaft refused to budge.

"Oh," said the teacher, "I forgot to tell you that the handle is in my pocket. Here it is."

The student slipped the handle over the shaft, easily turned it, and in a jiffy filled the glass with water. Nobody needed to tell the class what the aim of the lesson was. Each student wondered for himself why the all-too-familiar handle made such a difference— something that few had been aware of before. With curiosity aroused, all eyes were riveted on the teacher and all ears were wide open as the lesson about the wheel and axle as a basic machine proceeded.

This type of confrontation presents a real experience that contradicts or challenges an ordinary phenomenon with which students are thoroughly familiar. The unusualness challenges everyone to resolve the problem. They can only do so by investigating further, either by themselves or aided by the teacher's lesson.

Photographs also can provide confrontational motivation. Consider, for example, the two accompanying photographs. Show them on a screen with an overhead projector or in individual pictures or booklets.[1] Students describe mainly craters in picture A and plateaus or mounds in picture B. Ask them to invert the two photographs or the page. The appearance of the terrain in

---

[1] Hy Ruchlis. *Science Puzzle Pictures*. Brooklyn, N.Y.: Book-Lab, Inc., 1970.

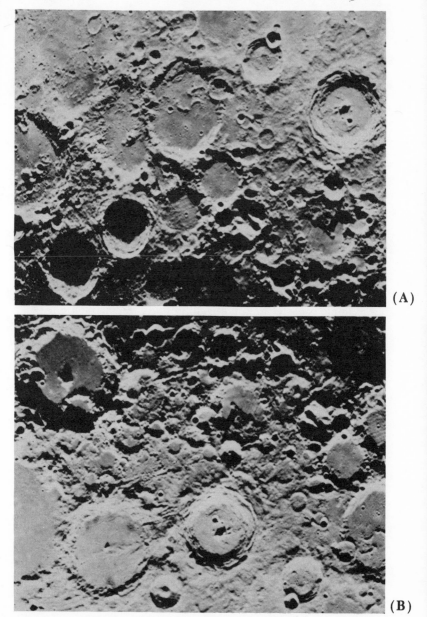

(A)

(B)

each photograph promptly reverses! (Try it by viewing the page upside down.) This surprising observation confronts students with evidence that they sometimes see things that are not so. Seeing is not necessarily believing. If they can be so confused by a seemingly simple observation, what assurance do they have about the validity of other more complex scenes, images, and events? This may lead to a discussion of human errors, mistaken observations, unreliability of witnesses' reports, and the general need for caution and care in reporting events.

Although such a lesson is obviously important for all students to learn, one troublesome aspect, typical of many reality-centered lessons, is that it does not readily fit into traditional subject categories. But the principle of things not always being what they seem can fit into many subjects—English, social studies, science, and art—if teachers so desire.

Good photographs of people or the environment can motivate many activities, especially in social studies and English classes. As an example consider the photograph of a jet taking off from Love Field in Dallas. This can generate a number of questions about the living conditions of people living nearby, the oily smoke in the air for miles, the noise pollution in the area, and so on.

Here is an example of confrontational motivation in mathematics. The teacher writes on the chalkboard:

$$
\left.\begin{array}{l}
1 + 1 = 10 \\
1 + 2 = 10 \\
1 \pm 3 = 10 \\
2 + 3 = 11 \\
4 + 3 = 12
\end{array}\right\} \quad \text{True or False?}
$$

These mathematical statements are false, but the teacher declares that they can be true. How is this possible? This real-life confrontation leads directly into a lesson about what 1 and 0 really mean when we write 10 and the basis for different number systems, of which the decimal system is but one of many. Thus, in the first statement $(1 + 1 = 10)$ the base could be 2, and 10 means one two and zero—a correct total. In the next statement (1

+ 2 = 10) the base could be 3 and the number 10 then would mean one three and zero.

An English lesson about punctuation might begin with the teacher writing on the chalkboard, "Time flies they go too fast" and confronting the class with the problem of determining the meaning of the statement. (If you are wondering about this yourself, the proper punctuation is: "Time flies? They go too fast!")

MOTIVATING WITH SONGS

Music and dance play an important role in the education of the very young, but by the fourth grade this type of activity generally stops. But the following song, sung on a record in a deep bass voice by Tom Glazer, illustrates motivational potential for eleven- or twelve-year-olds.

Why Does the Sun Shine?

The Sun is a mass of incandescent gas
A gigantic nuclear furnace
Where hydrogen is built into helium
At a temperature of millions of degrees

Yo ho, it's hot . . . the Sun is not
A place where we could live
But here on earth there'd be no life
Without the light it gives
We need its light, we need its heat
We need its energy
Without the sun without a doubt
There'd be no you and me

The Sun is a mass of incandescent gas
A gigantic nuclear furnace
Where hydrogen is built into helium
At a temperature of millions of degrees

The Sun is hot

(*It is so hot that everything on it is a gas: . . . Iron, copper,*
aluminum and many others are all gases).

The Sun is large

(*If the sun were hollow, a million earths could fit inside and*
yet, the sun is only a middle-sized star).

The Sun is far away

(*About 93,000,000 miles away and that's why it looks so*
small).

And even when it's out of sight
The sun shines night and day

The Sun gives heat, the Sun gives light—
The sunlight that we see
The sunlight comes from our own Sun's
Atomic energy

Scientists have found that the sun is a huge atom-smashing
machine. The heat and light of the sun come from the nu-
clear reactions of four comomn chemicals: hydrogen, carbon,
nitrogen and helium.

The Sun is a mass of incandescent gas
A gigantic nuclear furnace
Where hydrogen is built into helium
At a temperature of millions of degrees[2]

At first glance this song would seem to be about science and not
suitable for other subjects, but from a reality point of view, which
is always integrated with nature, the content can be related to a
variety of subjects. Of course, the song can be considered on its
own merits as music, but for the purpose of analysis, here are
some possible activities for regular subjects:

---

[2] Lyric by Hy Zaret   Music by Lou Singer   from Space Songs (Ballads For
The Age Of Science) copyright 1959 by Argosy Music Corporation.

English

Use the song to motivate vocabulary or spelling lessons emphasizing the following words or expressions:

mass	helium
incandescent	temperature
gigantic	aluminum
nuclear	reaction
furnace	chemical
hydrogen	nitrogen

Write a composition on the subject, "What do we know about the sun?" or "Without the sun there would be no you and me," or "A spaceship trip to the sun."

Compose your own poem about the sun.

Write a dramatic skit using a theme taken from the song.

Mathematics

How long would it take to reach the sun in a vehicle traveling one hundred miles an hour?

If the trip to the sun is to take one month (thirty days) at a steady speed, how fast would a spaceship have to travel?

If a million earths could fit into the sun, what is the diameter of the sun?

Art

Draw a picture illustrating a statement in the song or the entire song.

Design a mural illustrating the song.

Science

What do the following words or expressions in the song mean?:

mass	iron
incandescent	copper
gas	aluminum

nuclear	star
furnace	atomic energy
hydrogen	atom-smashing machine
helium	nuclear reaction
temperature	chemical
degrees	carbon
light	nitrogen
heat	

Could a spaceship land on the sun?

In what way is the sun like a nuclear furnace?

What would happen to us if the sun suddenly stopped giving heat and light?

What substances are found on the sun?

Can metals be gases?

Popular songs also offer a rich source of realistic sensory motivational material. For example, the "Sounds of Silence" by Paul Simon evokes feelings about loneliness in the big city, despite the crowds, glaring neon lights, and general hustle and bustle. The song can suggest questions about "What is progress?" "What good are material things?" and "Why are people lonely?" The poetic lyrics and melody place these questions in a very real setting.

Many activities may be generated around such a song, including writing poetry, illustrating the lyrics with drawings or photographs, or projecting photographs to illustrate the song as it is played on a record. Such activities cut across traditional subjects and can be pursued by various classes at the secondary level.

OTHER TECHNIQUES

An excellent motivational technique applicable to many lessons and units of study is encouraging students to brainstorm about a question raised by the teacher or by fellow students. The question must be of some consequence if it is to arouse interest. In other words, it must be perceived as a real question.

One general form of question suitable for many topics is, "What would happen if (X) did not exist (or stopped being produced, or was extremely scarce, or deteriorated)?" A specific example is, "Suppose that a virulent germ developed that fed on paper and was spread through the air by the winds. Suppose that no way of stopping the germ from spreading was found. What would happen to our civilization?"

The brainstorming would quickly reveal that civilization as we know it would be drastically altered, perhaps to the point of extinction. Without record keeping, bookkeeping, money, financial transactions, books, libraries, letters, newspapers, written and typed memos, cartons, boxes, or computer cards very drastic and costly measures would have to be taken to record information. The basic communication roles of written, typed, and printed messages would become clear as students brainstormed the question.

Supplementary questions could extend the discussion. For example, "How would loss of paper affect a mechanic fixing a car?" (He couldn't order a part from a catalog or look up the proper procedure for an unfamiliar repair in a technical manual.) "How would you pay for a new car (or house or groceries)?" "How would a judge, lawyers, and jury know what the law says?" "Could man go to the moon if there was no paper?" "Could your local supermarket continue to operate?"

Another general type of brainstorming question seeks solutions to current problems. "If you were in charge of solving (X) problem (the energy crisis, air pollution, war, mass transportation, reducing crime, construction of homes, improving cities, or improving education), what would you do?"

Brainstorming is most effective when questions deal with fundamental problems with which students can imaginatively and creatively eliminate nonessentials and get to the core of the matter. Brainstorming is a basic technique for reality-centered topics. By the same token, it is less effective and less often used in the kinds of courses that predominate in most schools today. Brainstorming never "sticks to the subject"—it cuts across the entire range of man's affairs in a highly divergent manner. It generates a broad overview of any reality-centered topic, which may then be studied in detail by more standard, convergent approaches.

Debates and panel sessions are similar devices that introduce a personal confrontation element that adds interest through clash of opinions. However, these techniques are not quite as informal as brainstorming in which everyone in the group is encouraged to contribute ideas. They require more preparation and are better suited to more mature students.

Role-playing is a motivation technique that can individualize a situation. Students are asked to imagine themselves in a particular setting and then act out what they feel are plausible reactions. Any real problem may easily be converted to a role-playing activity. The teacher presents a situation, preferably one in which there is a confrontational element, and then asks students to play out assigned roles.[3] The teacher may prepare the first few lines of a skit to develop a setting for a problem:

Owner of Glue-Making Factory: "Good morning. I understand that you wished to see me about something."
Committee Member A: "Yes. We want to talk to you about stopping the air pollution from your factory. The air smells so bad all day when the furnace is operating that we can't stay outdoors."
Committee Member B: "And the paint on our houses is stained by it. We have to paint every year."
Owner: "I know, and I am very sorry. I really sympathize with you. But I've looked into it, and it will cost two million dollars for new equipment. I just can't swing it. It would put me out of business. I would need help from the government."
. . . . (continued by participants)

---

[3] A number of suggestions for role-playing situations are offered in Bernard C. Hollister's "I Was Only Following Orders," *Media and Methods*, March 1974.

Role-playing is particularly useful for getting students to express their true feelings about controversial subjects and relationships among people, especially when their opinions are unpopular or they may fear the disapproval of the teacher. Students are always shielded from disapproval by the fact that they are only acting out a part. The technique tends to cut through the superficial layers of a problem to its raw essence.

Simulation games, which may also use role-playing approaches, are usually designed to enlighten students about complex social, political, and human relationships. It is difficult to design such games because to represent a real situation by means of instructions on cards or other symbolic means, one must pick and choose conditions from a variety of situations, thus omitting much reality. Also, acting according to printed instructions and tosses of dice, rather than in response to real-life circumstances, inevitably reduces the reality content. It is unlikely that most teachers could design effective games, except at the simplest level.

Nevertheless, good simulation games can have some positive features, particularly in cognitive areas that involve analysis, synthesis, making judgments and decisions, and evaluation. To some degree games may also be used to inform students about real aspects of economics, social and political procedures, and relationships in the world. A typical game of this type, Smog,[4] requires each of the players (up to four) to assume the role of the Air Quality Manager of a city. A "decision tree" is formed by each player to trace developments (determined by the throw of dice) that relate to zoning, population, industrial growth, and bids for federal funds. Players are constantly called upon to weigh and balance complex considerations and to make decisions and compromises involving voters with the purpose of achieving maximum air pollution control. Management credits are accumulated as various phases of the "decision tree" are completed, until one player

---

[4] Developed by Urban Systems, Inc., 1033 Massachusetts Ave., Cambridge, Mass. 02138.

accumulates 2,000 credits. In the course of playing such a game, a number of new terms and situations arise that may develop concepts related to pollution problems.

Simulation games provide opportunities to integrate content for students at different levels of cognitive development and also provide situations in which they may interact with each other in a more realistic relationship than is otherwise possible at school. Teachers can observe students and their reactions to a much wider range of new situations than are generally available in the classroom.

Since some types of simulation games are in an early stage of development or have not been adequately field tested with students of different abilities, it is wise to be cautious about accepting them uncritically from overenthusiastic authors or publishers. Many games have glaring faults. Most of those available require substantial blocs of class time, often more than is warranted by the situation being simulated. For example, one game that attempts to simulate presidential election campaigning calls for one hour of "presimulation discussion," not to speak of the time required for the teacher and players to master the many rules.

There is also the danger of becoming so enmeshed in the complex details, rules, logistics, and form filling required in some of the games that the entire thrust of the effort of teachers and students is diverted to merely playing the game, and the main educational purposes may be readily lost. Some games imply value-related concepts that are educationally questionable. In large part this defect stems from the use of chips and spinners and cards that seek to quantify the situation. One game, for instance, uses chips to buy and sell the "labor" of slaves and freemen without any indication that people with emotions and feelings are involved. The grandpa of simulation games, Monopoly, has this type of defect—players make and lose fortunes by means of maneuvers and manipulations that have no value-related concerns. It's as though some blind, inhuman genie turns a spinner, or throws a die, or picks a card that determines human choices and events. Since such negative value concepts and procedures are sufficiently objectionable, teachers should counteract their effects with appropriate discussion.

Recent research on the educational value of simulation games shows that they are no more effective in teaching content than regular teaching techniques, but they seem to have a positive influence on attitudes and motivation.[5] However, researchers have not yet fully evaluated the effect of simulation games on higher cognitive functions (analysis, synthesis, making judgments, and so on) nor have they evaluated the general effects on values and attitudes, e.g., there is the question of the effect that the process of playing games has on students. Is a competitive spirit fostered as opposed to cooperation? Do good game players tend to take over, submerging the leadership impulses of others?

In view of the pitfalls, it is wise for educators to seek objective classroom evaluations of simulation games before investing time and effort in what could prove to be negative educational activities. Where possible, it is best to have a group of students master a game on their own time to provide some preevaluation as well as to give a head start to overcoming the time-consuming mechanical obstacles of playing a game in class. It is also essential to avoid overusing simulation games, the way that some teachers and schools abuse films as time-fillers.

All in all, simulation games will probably have their greatest value in out-of-class activities, in clubs, study periods, at home, and similar student-centered activities, with the door held ajar for any that time and testing indicate may be effective for regular classroom use. If secondary school organization veers toward open classroom approaches, simulation games may be expected to play a larger role in motivating the study of various topics.

---

[5] Donald R. Wentworth and Darrell R. Lewis. "A Review of Research on Instructional Games and Simulations in Social Studies Education," *Social Education*, May 1973.

The specific examples of motivation noted in this chapter indicate how reality can play a large role in encouraging the desire for learning. Implementation in each subject is a matter not only for teachers but for curriculum makers. The authors hope that the examples cited will stimulate thinking about similar situations and additional techniques for motivating students to learn.

DEVELOPING 〽
CREATIVITY WITH 〽
DIVERGENT ACTIVITIES 〽

〽 Creativity is a human characteristic that plays a major role in man's ability to adapt to his environment and to change it; it is also a key force in many forms of art. On a smaller scale creativity helps individuals solve problems. Consequently, developing creativity should be a key goal of reality-centered education.

Unfortunately traditional education tends to neglect creative students, and they are generally left to fend for themselves outside the classroom.[1] Sometimes there is even direct conflict between creativity and school requirements as in the following instance.

A creative thirteen-year-old junior high school student submitted as his science project a study of background radioactivity in the atmosphere. He had counted the clicks recorded by a Geiger counter for five hundred fifteen-second intervals, determined that

---

[1] E. Paul Torrence. *Guiding Creative Talent*. Englewood Cliffs, N.J.: Prentice-Hall, 1962.

the occurrence of clicks was random, and by means of mathematics showed that the curve for the distribution of random clicks was a Poisson distribution (resembling a bell-shaped curve, but slanted sharply toward the lower values). He appeared before the committee of science teachers who were evaluating projects to be accepted for a borough-wide science fair. But they had a problem. A written report of this abstract research did not make a very flashy science fair display. Who would look at it? Nobody could press a button to make something move. So they asked the student what he "made." Did he, at least, make the Geiger counter? No, he did not. He had borrowed an inexpensive instrument. Well, then, said the committee, if he didn't make anything that could be displayed, they could not accept his report for the science fair. After all only a few openings were available. They couldn't send in a written project that had no accompanying equipment or large display and which therefore had no chance of winning a prize.

Naturally the creative student was furious. He felt that the entire procedure was not only unfair but, as he expressed it, "stupid." He would not have minded so much if the committee had not accepted his report because there were better projects, but the idea that rejection of a science project was based on a rule that students had to make something for display deeply violated his sense of justice. He lost his respect for the teachers who judged him and the system that held such distorted noncreative values.

The assumption is often made that a high IQ means bright and that this also implies creativity. In an investigation conducted by Jacob W. Getzels and Phillip W. Jackson, students in grades six through twelve were divided into two groups, one with high IQs but less creativity (as measured by a series of tasks) and another with lower (but above normal) IQs and high creativity.[2] Despite a twenty-three point difference in IQs, the two groups did equally well in their school careers. In general, Getzels and Jackson found low correlation between IQ and creativity. Considering the key

---

[2] *Creativity and Intelligence: Explorations with Gifted Students.* New York: John Wiley, 1962.

role IQ has played in determining student groupings for courses, it is apparent that schools are doing something wrong in this respect.

What is wrong is the failure to use the diversified teaching strategies, methods, and environments that cover the range of skills implied in creativity—thinking, producing, communicating, designing, planning, organizing, composing, risk-taking, exploring, imagining, fantasizing, and handling complex problems in a non-linear manner, all in a framework of persistent long-range effort.[3]

DIVERGENT VS CONVERGENT APPROACHES

The processes of human thought are many and varied, and no one simple description fits all cases. But there are very useful concepts that clarify how the mind works and are important for teachers to understand. Convergent and divergent activities are two complementary modes of thought that are closely related to learning styles and teaching methods and that are important in developing reality-centered, creative learning environments.

The differences between these modes of action and thought may be illustrated by the ways in which a scholar investigates a problem. Suppose he is studying an ancient chiselled stone record in a language not yet analyzed and is trying to crack the code. He searches all the crevices of his mind for clues to the strange writing. He may recall an image of a somewhat similar stone with similar chiselling, or formation of a figure, or material, or artistic style. He consults many books and articles and the published works of fellow scholars, probably over a long period of time. An idea pops into his head as he walks along the street or eats breakfast. He may mull it over and perhaps reject it or follow it up. He may attack the puzzle as one might a cryptogram, guessing what the meaning of a particular character might be and playing with it mentally until a pattern of relationships emerges.

After many years of such diverse, partially random activity—

[3] J. P. Guilford. "Roles of Structure-of-Intellect Abilities in Education," *Journal of Research and Development in Education*, Spring 1971, p. 4.

Figure 1: DIVERGENT ACTIVITY AND THINKING

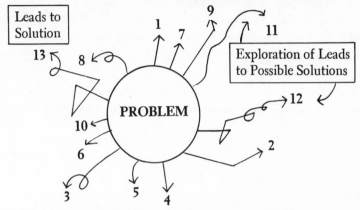

random in content as well as in time—one day the key idea that enables him to discover the basic clue to the meaning of the symbols comes to him, often seemingly out of nowhere.

Up to this point the major thrust of his activity and thinking— at least so far as its direction is concerned—has been divergent, moving outward from the central problem along relatively random paths, with much internal and external searching and many blind alleys (Figure 1). The entire range of his knowledge, skills, abilities, attitudes, values, and decision-making powers were brought to bear on the all-absorbing problem. In essence, the creative process is highly divergent in nature.

Recent research on the functions of the human brain indicate that, unlike all other animals, the left and right portions of man's brain have sharply differentiated functions.[4] The left half carries most of the load of verbal and logical thought, while the right half (whose functions are less clearly defined as yet) seems to specialize in the nonverbal aspects of thought—perception of shape, artistic appreciations, musical abilities, and perhaps the generally integrative creative realm of the mental processes. It is possible

---

[4] Maya Pines. "We Are Left-Brained or Right-Brained," *New York Times Magazine*, September 9, 1973.

that the right half of the brain may carry a greater share of the creative load during the divergent thinking process.

But after ideas have coalesced, it is necessary for the scholar, engineer, writer, manager, teacher, or scientist to communicate his or her conclusions to others in a logical, coherent manner, which can only be done through verbal or written means. Now the left half of the brain probably takes over the major role to present, in a convergent manner, the ideas in a logical one-two-three sequence rather than the helter-skelter order in which they originally occurred (Figure 2). The scholar marshalls all the applicable facts, principles, observations, and hypotheses, discards the non-essential ones and puts them all together in a tight, logical, neatly prepared package for all the world to read or perhaps to hear at a professional meeting. The process is reminiscent of Perry Mason presenting a convergent solution to the jury after the divergent travail of gathering together all the scattered clues. Of course, logical, convergent thinking was also done many times when the investigator tackled small bits of the problem that were susceptible to this mode of thinking. The work of most professionals entails a similar process.

Figure 2: CONVERGENT ACTIVITY AND THINKING

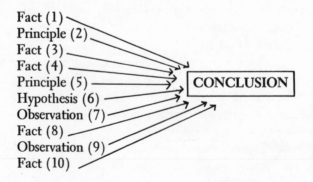

Many jobs and human activities are highly convergent, and some people prefer activities of this type. For example, a doctor treating a standard illness may, on the basis of a few clues, prescribe a series of routine tests and remedies with little or no divergent mind-searching. A teacher presenting a lesson he or she has taught many times will have no problem converging toward the immediate goal, assembling the required materials, and mapping out the sequence of almost predetermined questions. A scientist assigned the task of applying old techniques to a new area (for example, measuring the strengths of a new class of materials) will utilize mainly convergent approaches.

The creative portions of an activity require new approaches and divergent thinking, whereas traditional, customary activities require essentially convergent techniques. Schools should offer an appropriate balance between the two, a mix of divergent and convergent modes, that develops skills in both areas. For example, a lesson in a traditional science class might be based on the study of reflection of light (Figure 3). Since it begins with a convergent-style generalization, the contents of the lesson tend to be composed of convergent segments that form a tightly coherent whole. Divergent approaches tend to be minimal.

Figure 3: CONVERGENT ASPECTS
OF A TRADITIONALLY STRUCTURED LESSON

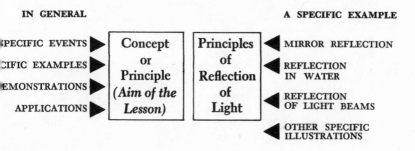

On the other hand, in real life one almost never observes reflection of light directly. When does one see rays of light bouncing off objects? Mirror images are observed, glare is noticed, and the moon is visible (by reflection of light), but unless one goes out of his way to actually bounce rays off a mirror, he will not see evidence of reflection of light. If teachers concentrate mainly on the abstract formulation of reflection of light, they and their courses are likely to lose sight of the real-life occurrences on which the concept is based. It required thousands of years of observation, divergent thought, and study before man learned the vital role reflection of light plays in visibility and in mirror images and expressed these properties in convergent-style generalized principles. It violates what we know about the stages of cognitive development to expect young people to bypass the basic pattern of discovery that led men to the generalized view of light rays bouncing off surfaces.

Judicious selection of experiences of discovery would help put some reality into the course by investigating real phenomena by divergent means (Figure 4). Consider as an example the specific case of a learning-by-doing lesson in which students are given a pair of mirrors and some procedural instructions for generating interesting observations. The main aim is not merely to learn specific facts about reflection of light but to promote doing skills and to provide learners an opportunity to generate their own ideas and follow them up. The fact that students can hold in their hands and manipulate an investigational object such as a mirror individualizes learning and makes an investigation meaningful and interesting.

DIVERGENT ACTIVITY WITH PEANUTS

An interesting characteristic of divergent activities is that their basic procedure may be adapted to many age levels. To illustrate this ageless quality, consider a lesson around the deceptively simple question, "What is the weight of a peanut?" Offhand, this question seems suitable only for younger students to teach them

Figure 4: DIVERGENT ASPECTS OF INVESTIGATION
OF AN INTERESTING OBJECT,
PHENOMENON OR EVENT

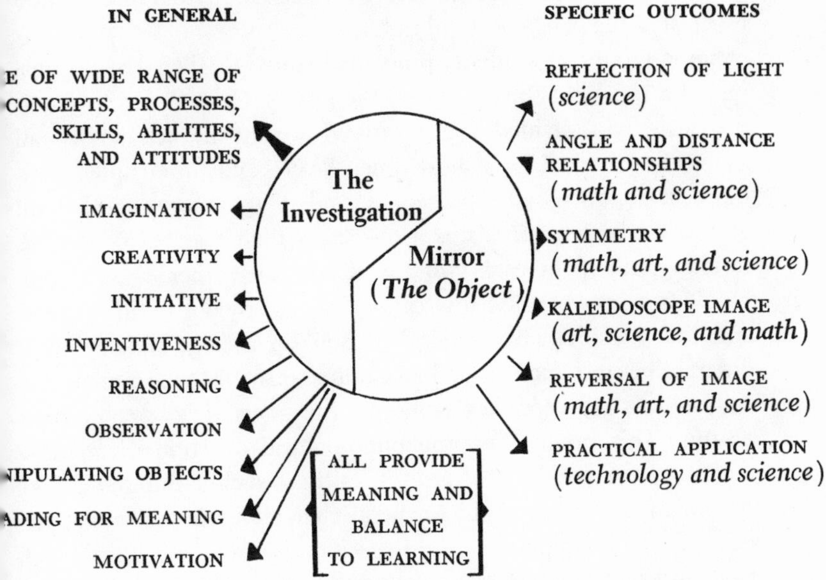

IN GENERAL

E OF WIDE RANGE OF
CONCEPTS, PROCESSES,
SKILLS, ABILITIES,
AND ATTITUDES

IMAGINATION

CREATIVITY

INITIATIVE

INVENTIVENESS

REASONING

OBSERVATION

NIPULATING OBJECTS

ADING FOR MEANING

MOTIVATION

The
Investigation

Mirror
(*The Object*)

[ALL PROVIDE
MEANING AND
BALANCE
TO LEARNING]

SPECIFIC OUTCOMES

REFLECTION OF LIGHT
(*science*)

ANGLE AND DISTANCE
RELATIONSHIPS
(*math and science*)

SYMMETRY
(*math, art, and science*)

KALEIDOSCOPE IMAGE
(*art, science, and math*)

REVERSAL OF IMAGE
(*math, art, and science*)

PRACTICAL APPLICATION
(*technology and science*)

how to use a weighing device. But the following describes an
actual lesson at the college level based on this question.

The activity was conducted in a class for prospective science
teachers (college seniors and graduates) to illustrate the difference between a reality-centered divergent science laboratory lesson and one in a traditional style. The class was divided into
groups of two or three, each of which was presented with an equal-
arm balance (the kind that has two equally distant pans on opposite sides of the pivot) and ten peanuts and asked to find,
"What is the weight of a peanut?"

Announcement of this apparently ⋅ simple problem produced
laughter—after all, these were mature, science-trained adults.
Finding the weight of a peanut seemed ridiculously easy.

The catch was that the teacher wasn't asking for the weight of a
specific peanut; instead the question implied finding the weight of
a *generalized* peanut, which presumably would represent or approximate *all* peanuts. Also, the teacher had surreptitiously turned

the adjustment knobs on the scales to put the pans slightly off balance. Several students noticed the unequal original balance and readjusted the pans; most did not.

Some groups of students proceeded to weigh their ten peanuts one at a time and then averaged the results. Others put all ten on the scale and divided the measured weight by ten. After all groups had worked for a short time, the class was interrupted for a moment to discuss the procedure, and it was suggested that all groups try both methods as a check on their results. When the results produced by each group were compared, there were significant differences because the scales were slightly out of adjustment and the measurements and calculations of average weights were different because each group had a different set of ten peanuts.

The class still couldn't agree on the *generalized* weight of a peanut. This brought up the philosophical question of what is meant by the weight of *a* peanut. Is there such a thing as a real peanut in the abstract? The general characteristics can be identified only by averaging based on specific cases, but we still do not have an exact description of the weight of any specific peanut in general.

In an attempt to get a more accurate estimate, the class collated the data gathered by all groups. It became apparent that there was a statistical distribution of weights of individual peanuts, with the values for weights bunching around a central mode and tailing off at each extreme—the familiar bell-shaped curve. They were getting into advanced mathematics; the weight of *a* peanut became even more remote. It became necessary to make a statistical analysis of the data to even approximate an answer to the question.

What seemed at the beginning a very simple, definite problem was actually highly divergent and open-ended and gradually became more and more involved, complex, and difficult. Why did it have these qualities? First, real balances and peanuts, not abstract ones, were used, and all students had a real and individual experience, even in a thirty-to-one classroom. Second, the problem was stated in very general terms, not in the usual specific, limited one in which most of the open-endedness and discovery potential would have disappeared.

It would have been better to have had the students discover and state their own problem, but the original problem generated its own new problems, which were personally encountered in a confrontational manner and therefore became the students' problems. The lesson was planned to introduce this divergent characteristic.

For younger students a preliminary lesson on the use of scales might be essential. Even so, it would be best not to give step-by-step instructions, and it would be desirable to allow the youngsters to fumble a bit, as they would in any new situation in real life, thereby generating the need for instruction. That would spark motivation to learn from a real experience, with a high degree of individualization.

This activity required a substantial block of time, at a much more leisurely pace than is traditional. Such unhurried allotments of time are essential to develop the inherent potentials of a divergent activity and for the self-pacing required for individualized learning. The basic teaching procedure in this instance was relatively informal. In the main, it was up to the students to work out their procedures, and they discovered for themselves new directions for open-ended activity. Such a lesson required many skills and cut across traditional subjects (science, mathematics, philosophy) to integrate learnings. All these characteristics are typical of divergent lessons and tend to balance the formality and single-mindedness of customary convergent lessons.

DIVERGENT ACTIVITY WITH "SCRIBBLES"

The following activity, which integrates art and writing, illustrates how a divergent type of learning-by-doing activity can develop skills involving creativity, imagination, and initiative. As is characteristic of many divergent activities, the general procedure is applicable to a range of age and conceptual levels. In this instance the activity described is for grades five to nine, but it could be adapted to grades two through adult.[5]

Students are asked to draw a random scribble across a sheet of paper (Figure 5). They then observe their scribbles from different viewpoints, turning the paper as necessary and searching for shapes resembling objects or, preferably, animals or people. Areas of the design are then blocked out to produce a picture and colored with crayons (Figure 6). The teacher then suggests that the scribble drawing serve as the inspiration for imaginative, free-association poems or compositions or discussion. What is the person or animal or thing doing? How did he or she or it get that way? Tell a story about him, her, or it.

The original randomly curved scribble line generally possesses a natural flow that sets up a graceful framework for a drawing. The randomness introduces very divergent characteristics because each person makes a different scribble each time (and a different drawing and different story) and secondly, because the search for significant features in the scribble involves a divergent process of selection. The choice of features depends on a combination of subconscious clues, the particular perceptions of the observer, and

Figure 5: A TYPICAL "SCRIBBLE"

Figure 6: A THREE-HEADED MONSTER

---

[5] This activity was developed by Phyllis Rubin, now a teacher of a sixth-grade class at a Brooklyn school.

perhaps her or his mood at the moment. Similarly the story or poem tends to be highly divergent and uninhibited because of the setting in which the drawing is made.

Here, for example, is a typical poem by a fifth grader. The scribble drawing upon which it is based is shown in Figure 7.

CAREY MARY

Miss Carey Mary
Was walking down the street
When she found
A witch standing by her feet.

The witch put a spell
On poor Carey Mary
She was more sad
Than a non-speaking canary.

Miss Carey Mary
Was ugly and fat
And that is why she put on
Her funny looking hat.

Figure 7: MISS CAREY MARY

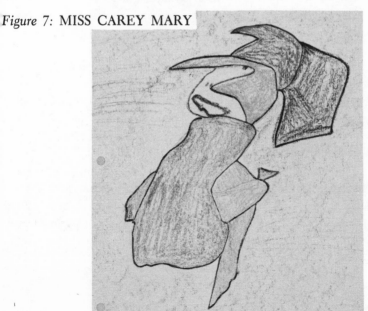

Schools traditionally tend to exclude subconscious, free flowing imaginative approaches that are a natural part of thought and action, but the imaginative art and writing of young people are very real to them. Activities such as these that allow students to exercise their imaginations should be encouraged.

INVENTING GAMES

The world of games is quite familiar and enjoyable to students. Inventing and hand-producing new games requires divergent processes and integration of knowledge and skills, particularly if the games are to be used for some worthwhile purpose, such as gifts for children in a local hospital or for sale at low prices in a student co-op store. This judgment is based on experiences with such an activity with a group of teenagers at a Mobilization for Youth Center in the Lower East Side of Manhattan; most of the young people were not successful in school and generally felt that they were incapable of achievement. The major educational objective of this experiment was to provide ways of developing a positive self-image by accomplishment in a significant area. There was an important element of reality in this activity—these youngsters were paid, mostly from federal funds, and their job was to produce games to sell at the co-op store.

After several exploratory sessions and considerable hesitation in undertaking what seemed to them too difficult a task, the ice was broken when one group of boys developed a sentence game with some help from the instructor. Thereafter, these supposedly unsuccessful students produced a flood of new educational games that had considerable originality and utility.

Problems of producing the games provoked animated discussions and touched upon many practical activities as well as subjects in the curriculum. For example, the sentence game raised questions like these: "Should the game be made of paper or cardboard?" "How many cards will be needed?" "How large should they be for easy handling?" "How could they be laid out economically on sheets of cardboard?" "Should the forms be mimeographed or made by hand?" "What method should we use to make them efficiently in moderate quantities?" The designers become aware of the need for selecting a proper proportion of nouns, verbs, and other parts of speech to make the game playable. They agreed that about one hundred cards would be suitable. But then, "Can we afford to put so many 3 × 5 inch file cards into each game?" "Could we use smaller cards and cut costs?" The students were given a sheet of paper and asked to imagine that it was a large card to be cut into smaller cards, each with a word on it. The number of cards and their arrangement on the sheet could be determined by folding the paper. A size about 1¼ × 2½ inches was agreed upon. There was also some animated discussion about a name for the game.

The need for instructions became apparent, and writing them gave considerable opportunity for language development. Discussion was essential to work out ideas within a group and to explain them to others. Writing an assigned composition is a private matter between student and teacher, and there is little motivation for a student who never expects to use this kind of skill, but writing rules for a game that others will use is a totally different matter. Students know the written rules must be clear and comprehensible. No author wants to publish work that is improperly spelled and grammatically incorrect, and students who want to publish rules for a game are in the same position—their published rules must be correct, and they realize the need for working to make them so.

Mathematical concepts entered into design and use of many of the games. Counting, addition, and subtraction are necessary for scoring. Game boards generally involve geometrical constructions, measurement, and computation, and competent art work is an asset.

No doubt one could encourage interest in geography, history, and other subjects by suggesting the invention of games in these subjects. The divergent activity of inventing educational games involves young people in the educational process directly and individually, not as passive learners but as active participants. Inventing and producing games also provides an achievable goal and requires a variety of skills beginning with the origin of the idea all the way to design and production.

A CLASS NEWSPAPER

One of the best ways to introduce divergent processes as well as reality into learning to read and write is to have the class produce a newspaper in which all students can see their own words in print, headed with a by-line. Contributions may be long or short, a poem or a joke, a puzzle or a riddle, a comment or an essay. They may be self-generated or suggested by the teacher, and authors may write by themselves or receive help with ideas and spelling.

Few activities offer stronger motivation for learning to write and spell. It is one thing to write a sentence or composition for the teacher to mark, but quite another to have everybody read it for personal enjoyment. No young person wants the world to know that he or she spells poorly. If they need help, they will go out of their way to find it. And they will be proud to take the newspaper home to show their families; they may even sell it to neighbors.

The cost of printing two hundred copies of a class newspaper with the aid of student squads and easy-to-operate printing machines or modern duplicators is minimal. Few activities can match it in terms of integrating subject content, motivation, exercise of initiative and creativity, and a sense of reality.

CONCRETE OR ABSTRACT: 🎶
THE ROLE OF 🎶
THE SENSES 🎶

🎶 To newborn babies the real world consists of specific objects that they can feel, see, and hear and specific events that they experience. But, with the passage of time and accumulation of experiences, a child develops along the stages so aptly described by Piaget—generalizing from concrete sensory experience and assembling abstract conceptual patterns of increasing complexity. Despite this constant development of abstraction throughout the school years, one must never forget that the base of most learning is sensory experience. We read with our eyes. We listen to discussions with our ears. We write with our hands, coordinating them with sensory impressions in our eyes. The basic tools for learning abstract concepts are the senses, and it is well known that defective senses usually lead to defective learning.

By and large, educators underestimated the importance of relating learning to the senses, particularly for younger children, and move too rapidly into abstract areas. We must take young children as they are and approach them mainly through their senses, with a high proportion of concrete, multisensory impressions. Later, as they develop a framework of concepts, a larger proportion of abstract approaches can be utilized, but even so, the concrete and down-to-earth specifics of a subject should never disappear altogether in the teaching process.

Underestimating the effect of concrete sensory experience is an important reason for the learning failure of many students at secondary levels. Frequently shifting from abstract to concrete approaches is a way to put a student back on the learning track. In the days before language labs French or Spanish was learned mainly from books, and when students eventually visited France or Spain, they couldn't understand the language spoken by its native practitioners—although they might read a newspaper with some degree of success. The assumption that one could learn to speak a language by reading and writing it had little merit—direct sensory experience with speech is essential to mastery of it.

When students fail a subject despite a desire to learn, the difficulty is most often due to content and methodology that is too abstract for them. The obvious remedy is to make the content more real by decreasing its abstractness and increasing sensory experience. It is possible, of course, to tell someone what has been discovered about rain, or the Plains Indians, or the stars, and past events can often be dramatized to convey what one has not personally experienced. But, where possible, an actual sensory experience clarifies what is being discussed and provides motivation for learning—especially for younger or failing students. If that is not possible, substitutes in the form of films, pictures, or role-playing can be effective.

Consider a situation that might be faced by an explorer who reaches a remote tropical island. He attempts to explain ice skating to the natives, and they listen in astonishment as he regales them with tales of water that becomes as hard as a rock and of people who put on shoes with sharp blades and glide about on the surface of the hardened water. What do the inhabitants of the tropical island think about all this? More likely than not they are extremely skeptical or unable to conceive of ice at all. But one trip to the arctic and its frozen seas would give the islanders a real, experiential basis for understanding the nature of frozen water and its relation to temperature. Or a direct experience with the formation of ice in a refrigerator could substitute for such a trip.

Students are often in a similar predicament when learning a new subject. Much of what they are taught lies beyond their experience, and the abstract things they are told in some of their lessons must seem as strange and as difficult to understand as ice skating would be to tropical islanders.

A READING PROCESS

In secondary schools today there are significant numbers of teenagers who have little or no ability to read. Some are so far behind that they may read a word such as *can* as *cat* or may not even know all the letters of the alphabet. This problem seems insolvable and hopeless to many secondary school teachers because of the continuous failure by these nonreaders over so many crucial years. Actually there is considerable evidence, based on experience, that most nonreaders can improve substantially if the concrete-sensory content of the lessons is increased. A method of teaching reading, developed by Dr. Cecelia Pollack of Herbert H. Lehman College of the City University of New York, is of considerable interest in this discussion. A major emphasis of her *Intersensory Reading Program*[1] is to increase the concrete-sensory content of the specific procedures used to correct basic deficiencies.

For many children in the first grade, the customary introduction to the ABCs and word structure is too great a conceptual leap for intellectual comfort; in other words, it is too abstract for them.

---

[1] *Intersensory Reading Program.* Brooklyn, N.Y.: Book-Lab, Inc., 1967.

These children learned to speak effectively and to communicate with others using complex sound combinations purely by imitation, in most cases without any conscious attempt to analyze the structure of words and with no experience in relating spoken words to printed or written symbols. But "readiness" for reading and writing imply that the learners have developed a number of abstract concepts and abilities upon which instruction must be based. They must have developed sufficient auditory perception to be able to recognize the separate sounds in a word. Although a word such as *man* is a single unit in terms of speech and meaning, for purposes of reading and writing it must be analyzed into its three separate sound elements, *m*, *a*, and *n*. If this skill is lacking, learners will be unable to synthesize letters to form words. Learners must also understand the difference between left and right and up and down, so that they will not reverse the positions of letters such as *b*, *p*, and *d*. They must be able to distinguish long lines from short ones as with *n* and *h*. They must be able to distinguish between different kinds of shapes so they will recognize the subtle differences between letters. Without such auditory and visual perception skills, learners have little hope of benefitting from reading instruction.

To illustrate the process of teaching teenage nonreaders to overcome their handicaps, consider the extreme case of a fourteen-year-old boy who totally lacked the ability to observe that the word *man* consisted of three parts—*m*, *a*, and *n*. Dr. Pollack's method of handling such a boy begins at a concrete level below the customary ABCs. The visual problems of recognizing letters of the alphabet printed on a page are temporarily sidetracked by using real objects as symbols to represent sounds. When one actually holds an object, it is a much more real and concrete experience than seeing a symbol. It is easy for a nonreader to understand that a comb may represent the hard *k* sound of the letter *c*, that a toy apple may represent the short vowel sound of *a*, and that a toy table may represent the sound of *t*. The word *cat* may then be symbolically represented by placing the comb, apple, and table in a left to right sequence, pronouncing the separate sound elements, and then blending them into the spoken word *cat*. The kinesthetic sensations involved in placing the objects on the desk reinforce learning the object-symbols and left-right relationships; they seem closer to some learners' basic sensory equipment and feelings of reality than the visual perceptions involved in recognizing the shapes of letters.

The seemingly hopeless fourteen-year-old nonreader who began the learning process by manipulating object-symbols representing letters soon grasped the concept and learned to identify the separate sounds of simple words. This knowledge was then transferred to visual letters on cards, which were substituted one-by-one for the object-symbols, and the student was soon spelling simple words with the letter cards and learning the letters of the alphabet. Soon he progressed to extremely simple reading selections that used very few letters.[2] The first selection, for example, used only four letters of the alphabet. At this stage instruction included a high degree of sensory involvement; reading, writing, and dictation produced maximum intersensory (visual-auditory-kinesthetic) reinforcement.

Gradually the instruction shifted from emphasis on the concrete to increased use of the abstract. Within sixteen months this seemingly hopeless nonreader progressed to a fourth-grade reading level, read simple newspaper stories, and began to move into the mainstream of the educational process. He set his sights on completing his education at an automotive trades school. Furthermore, former severe psychological problems in which his inability to read played a major role were well on the way to being resolved.

This dramatic rescue was not brought about just by appropriate use of a methodology featuring concrete content but involved a complex of psychological and educational techniques. Nevertheless, understanding the relationship of concrete to abstract played

[2] Cecelia Pollack and Patrick R. Lane. *The Hip Reader*. Brooklyn: Book-Lab, Inc., 1970.

an important role in the achievement. The use of concrete experiences in this case also illustrates reality-centered instruction. Reality content for the nonreader was enhanced with reading selections that dealt with the lives of teenagers in a similar environment, with photographic illustrations with which the learner could identify. Even the title of the book—*The Hip Reader*—added reality for a normally antagonistic learner.

ANOTHER EXAMPLE—JUDGMENT OF WEIGHT

To illustrate the role of concrete experience at a considerably higher educational level, consider the following experiment, which can be conducted at any level from ninth grade through graduate school.

The class is presented with the "simple" problem of comparing the weight of two objects by hand to determine which is heavier. One object is compact and dense, for instance, a steel ball about ¾ to 1 inch in diameter or a one- or two-ounce lead sinker. The other object is large and light, for example, a styrofoam block or empty box about the size of a brick and weighing slightly more than the compact, dense object. If the large object is lighter than the compact, dense object, increase its weight by taping small objects to it in a way that they are hidden from view. A scale will be required, preferably the equal-arm balance type, although a postal scale can serve.

The teacher holds up both objects and asks which is heavier. A student is given the two objects, one in each hand, and asked to quickly compare their weight. A response such as, "The metal ball is about twice as heavy" is typical, although occasionally a response of, "Five times as heavy" for the ball will be forthcoming. More rarely a student will say, "They are equal." It is most unusual for anyone to say that the large object is heavier; later discussion usually reveals that such a response was solely an attempt to be different. Whatever response is given is accepted, and the teacher writes a list of numbers from one to twenty on the chalkboard to record the responses given by students as each holds the objects. The objects are passed around the room for everybody in the class to compare weights—an essential element of the sensory experience featured in this lesson.

Every group has a different pattern of response in accordance with the conformity effect—much depends on the first few judgments, which generally set an overall pattern. Usually responses will cluster between two and six times as heavy for the metal object, with occasional higher values up to and beyond ten. Occasionally someone will go up to twenty, especially if this number is listed on the board.

Discussion of the observations rapidly elicits the opinion that the senses are not very accurate at comparing weights, but the class will agree, at least, that they can still tell which is heavier. The teacher then brings out the balance and compares the weights of the objects. The equal-arm balance is most dramatic because the comparison is immediate, with the side containing the heavier object going down.

Students will be astonished and will not believe it. Since their senses informed them that the compact object was heavier, and this judgment is almost always unanimous, it seems impossible for *all* to be wrong. "Perhaps the scale is wrong?" Students quickly suggest that this possibility be tested by switching sides. The large object still goes down on the scale. The shock of the class must be seen to be believed. To a considerable extent this drama occurs because students have felt the weights themselves and have participated personally in making a judgment based on their perception —a judgment that proves to be wrong.

The reality of this experience may be pursued in divergent directions with outcomes that touch upon measurement, physics, biology, psychology, and philosophy. For example, if a teacher wants to use this activity to illustrate the conformity effect, it is effective to postpone the actual weighing until after a discussion about why students rendered the judgments they did. As one student once said, "I would have said twelve times as heavy, but the highest judgment up to then was three times as heavy. I only said five." Another might declare, "I said the weights were equal, even though I felt the ball to be two or three times as heavy, because I figured you were trying to fool us."

Physics and biology are involved in the explanation of the phenomenon. The compact, dense object exerts force on a very small area of the palm, and the pressure is higher. The nerves in the palm sense pressure, not weight, and the signals they send to the brain are misinterpreted to mean weight. The latter point in turn touches on psychology. Philosophy can enter into the discussion through exploration of the question, "How can we be sure of a fact?" There is also a more immediate point—the need for objective measurement devices to make accurate judgments and comparisons.

Dramatic, personal experiences of this kind that directly involve the senses provide excellent motivation for certain types of learning, as anyone who has touched a hot stove or inserted a finger into an open electrical socket with the current on has discovered. At a higher level, a budding poet may be motivated by smelling a rose or by the visual impressions of a beautiful girl walking along the street. Of course, sensory impressions are not essential for all learning, particularly at upper levels where abstractions play an increasingly important role. But, for effective learning for most students, most of the time, and especially for younger students or those who are having difficulties with a subject, nothing takes the place of personal sensory involvement in an experience of interest or importance. Concrete personal experience utilizing sensory information also helps individualize learning.

This weight-judging activity can be used to illustrate Piaget's findings to groups of teachers or student teachers. The inability of adults to compare small weights accurately is due to lack of experience with such phenomena. The other skills they have developed do not contribute very much to this particular task—in fact, their specific past experiences may contribute to their being misled in this instance. Teachers who experience such a total failure of judgment of weight may be more sympathetic toward a child who is inept in any particular skill by virtue of his or her inexperience with it.

HEY THERE, DOWN BELOW!

One of the basic factors that increases abstract content and diminishes concreteness and reality at all levels is the organization of education into levels, with distinct areas for elementary, junior and senior high, and college. This encourages teachers to adjust instruction at each level to what is expected at the next level. Education is often viewed as climbing a ladder, with students constantly progressing up the rungs of achievement, with college as the ultimate goal. Such a mindset causes curriculum designers to select content at lower levels that is excessively abstract in the effort to prepare children for upper levels. There is a tendency to neglect the reality of children's real educational needs at the lower levels in favor of what is expected of them later. This practice probably contributes to the traumatic failure of about twenty percent of the children in the early grades who fail to learn to read effectively. Even a cursory examination of most courses of study at higher levels indicates that much of the content is very abstract and based upon hasty, one-sided covering of ground to prepare students for the next higher level.

It would be more realistic to view educational progression as a walk on terra firma toward a distant goal rather than climbing up a ladder. The ladder view makes any specific rung unimportant—only the end result counts. The rungs are the means to the end. One cannot stop and relax on a rung but must work steadily to reach the top. But if one takes a horizontal walk to a goal, it is possible to relax and enjoy all portions of the trip without undue strain. And if there are interesting things to be seen along the way, one can stop a bit to investigate. Perhaps it is the ladder concept of education that causes so many college graduates to stop all further academic learning, or even reading, once they have obtained a degree. They feel entitled to rest after such a strenuous journey. But with the horizontal walk concept, if the trip is reasonably pleasant and the goal is achieved, might a hiker not like to take another excursion at the next opportunity?

There is a widespread propensity for teachers at each level of instruction to complain about "what goes on down below." Constructive criticism and closer communication between levels are always welcome and can be most helpful. But all teachers, at any level, must work with the actual reality of their students and their school environment. No teacher should be afraid to teach about some important aspect of the students' environment because somebody later on will complain about the wrong ideas they picked up. Many ideas at a lower level are "wrong" in some respect when viewed from a higher level of learning. Teachers at higher levels of abstraction must work with what they get and continually polish the rough edges of inevitably immature concepts. They, too, will get their comeuppance from teachers at a still higher level who will complain about the poor material being sent up from below.

Some purists do not realize learners' needs to have difficult abstract concepts simplified. Teachers may become fearful of being inexact and criticized when they simplify principles, and they omit some concepts to be on safer ground. Much of the failure of teachers to explore new areas and to teach new topics by "doing" stems from this fear of being wrong in some respect. Teachers and curriculum makers at all levels should practice what scientists do successfully—advance by a series of improved approximations to the truth and to reality.

THE REALITY
BASE FOR
VALUES

✿ Inculcating values and attitudes is probably the most difficult educational goal to achieve, especially at a time when young people are questioning the basic values of society. To some extent failures in this area are due to the valid fear that once teachers begin to stress what they think are proper values, it is easy to overstep the limits into "big brother" education and develop robots who simply think as they are told. One of the authors recalls the surprise of a group of teachers, who had been complaining about the disobedience and lack of discipline in their schools, when an ex-German refugee, listening attentively to the discussion, blurted out, "I don't know about that. I saw the terrible things obedient, orderly people did under Hitler. I don't think that could happen too easily in America where every kid tells you where to get off."

In the recent past, teaching values and attitudes was not stressed because it was associated with the fire-and-brimstone, hell-

and-damnation variety of preaching. Teachers tried to avoid (and still do) getting into hassles over whether or not what they taught was violating popular opinion. Experience with "preaching" values clearly indicates that most young people today are turned off by such an approach.

Another major share of the responsibility for failure in teaching values undoubtedly rests with the traditional subject orientation of the curriculum. When abstract subjects such as French, American history, geometry, or biology are studied, attention is focused on subject content and not on values that are difficult to test for on examinations.

The thirty-to-one classroom organization and tests and grades also inhibit development of appropriate value systems; in fact, they tend to encourage some undesirable values. Fellow students often appear to be competitors, particularly when teachers mark on a curve, and a student can rise only by kicking someone else downstairs. One may argue that the work-a-day world consists of bosses and workers, and teacher-student relationships that resemble this reality are more likely to prepare students for their adult roles. However, the existing dominant mode of classroom organization militates against desirable values such as cooperation and respect for others, and some modification is needed.

ROLE OF SCHOOLS IN DEVELOPING VALUES

There is a feeling among some educators and many citizens that the development of values—often referred to as moral values—is the responsibility of the home and the church, not the schools. But, since school is a major part of the environment for all the young, from ages five or six to sixteen or more, it is inevitable that their experiences there will play an important role in framing their value systems, for better or worse, whether we like it or not. The schools cannot dodge responsibility for strengthening positive values and must accept blame when their failures weaken desirable values.

Inside the schools initially well-adjusted children may learn from their peers how to cheat, steal, gang up on other kids, play dirty tricks, break windows, or smash up chairs. They may learn from their coaches that winning the game is the most important objective, no matter what they must do to win. On the other hand, maladjusted children from unfortunate home environments may improve their value systems (from society's viewpoint) by experiencing cooperation, respect, and help from teachers and peers. Much depends upon the situation within the school and its relationship to the local environment.

An individual's value system begins to develop in infancy from the pattern of values experienced at home and in the social environment. The pattern may develop by extension and growth or by change to a new direction. Three desirable phases have been noted in a hierarchy of value changes:[1]

1. Choosing from alternatives: This must be done freely, preferably after thoughtful consideration of the consequences.
2. Prizing the value: The person is happy with the choice and is willing to affirm it publicly.
3. Acting on the basis of the value: The value leads to action, or actions are affected by the value judgment.

It is difficult, if not impossible, for teachers to help students develop desirable values if they approach the matter in an authoritarian way. True opinions are not expressed unless discussions are completely democratic, without pressures to conform, with freedom to state thoughts, and with the right to disagree. Dissenting opinions often represent the first stage in resolving an internal conflict and do not necessarily mean that students who express them have their minds permanently set on the value they proclaim.

Values and valuing are personal, often gradual, accommodations to new ideas, attitudes, and beliefs, and it is unreasonable to expect that any one or few discussions will resolve conflicts once

---

[1] Louis Raths et al. *Values and Teaching: Working with Values in the Classroom.* Columbus: Charles E. Merrill, 1966.

and for all. The purpose of discussion is to introduce students to alternatives to be considered. Often this is best done by questions that elicit self-analysis of values and clarify one's true position. Some useful questions that serve this purpose are: "Do you care about that?" "What do you mean by that (nonbelligerently)?" "Have you considered alternatives?" "Does that idea suggest changes in the way we should treat people?"

The process of clarification avoids moralizing, criticizing, insisting on teachers' values, or evaluating ideas presented by students as good, bad, or acceptable. However, teachers should accept the responsibility for helping students weigh and discuss such issues as the need for laws in society.

One of the major realities for half the student population—the girls—is that they are subjected to many subtle pressures to conform to old concepts of women as secondary partners of men, whose primary functions are to stay home, bear children, keep the home fires burning, and to follow and support whatever careers their menfolk may pursue. The impact of the women's liberation movement has accelerated the loosening of restrictions on women and is changing their status to one of full equality with men.

Teachers now have a special dual responsibility to develop new values for both girls and boys. First, it is necessary to raise the sights of girls by providing experiences that give them feelings of true equality with boys. Secondly, boys must realize that girls are their full equals in both potential and accomplishment. Girls should be encouraged to take shop courses on an equal basis with boys and to participate in team sports on an equivalent merit basis. The arbitrary banning of girls from team sports must be stopped—such practices are now illegal.

Teachers must change their own attitudes and behavior to deal with these new realities. For example, does a male teacher prefer girl secretaries to boys? Are only boys selected to carry books? When discussing occupations, is it assumed that only boys can become pilots or doctors? Is it taken for granted that only girls will be interested in courses in cooking and fashion design? During discussions of the family and social structure, is it tacitly assumed that the major role of women is running the home? Does the teacher discuss sexist practices that inhibit girls from expressing their full potential as leaders? Do teachers expose the usual contemptuous attitudes boys have toward girls' potential careers and abilities? Do they encourage girls to express their potentials fully and help them to enter the mainstream of modern life without the psychological handicaps of the past?

Although the staff of a school does not, except in a peripheral way, determine the pattern of values embraced by a community, it does have some degree of control over the general atmosphere and tone within the school and its influence on value systems. A major function of any school administration is to create an atmosphere that fosters desirable values and attitudes. It achieves this goal by operating schools democratically, fairly, cooperatively, and humanely for both students and teachers. The administration may even encourage teachers and students to address themselves to values and attitudes with stimulating programs, faculty meetings, and curriculum modifications.

Teachers can develop classroom environments in which positive values are exemplified. Haim Ginott has described his power as a teacher to create a constructively valued environment in the classroom or a destructively valued one.

> I've come to a frightening conclusion that I am the decisive element in the classroom. It's my personal approach that creates the climate. It's my daily mood that makes the weather. As a teacher, I possess a tremendous power to make a child's life miserable or joyous. I can be a tool of torture or an instrument of inspiration. I can humiliate or humor, hurt or heal. In all situations, it is my response that decides whether a crisis will be escalated and a child humanized or dehumanized.[2]

---

[2] "Driving Children Sane," *Today's Education*, November–December 1973, p. 25.

Dr. Ginott went on to describe a classroom conversation that illustrates how a teacher may provide a negative model.

A boy had lost his pencil and said to his teacher, "Teacher, I lost my pencil."

The teacher responded:

"John, did you lose your pencil?" This, after the child had just told him, "I lost my pencil."

"I'd like to know what you did with it."

"Did you eat it?"

"What happened to it?"

"What color was it?"

"You can't do your work without a pencil."

"I'll get you a pencil."

"Make sure the pencil is here tomorrow."

"And don't tell me tomorrow that you lost this pencil too."

Nine statements and all of them unnecessary. If the teacher was going to give the boy a pencil, he should have given it graciously. "Here is another pencil, Johnny." At least the teacher would receive a thank you and would be able to say, "You're welcome."[3]

In this instance the teacher has served as a model of a sarcastic, authoritarian, and uncooperative husband or wife, salesclerk, or civil service worker. Students learn values in the classroom mainly by the concrete examples the teacher and the other students provide. Preaching is not only much less effective but is also generally counterproductive.

TECHNIQUES FOR DEVELOPING ACTIVITIES

Over and above general considerations of atmosphere and tone, how can teachers tackle values directly in the classroom? Is this an undesirable or impossible task to be avoided?

---

[3] Ibid.

There are values and attitudes that are relatively noncontroversial—cooperative attitudes, respect for others, democratic modes of acting and thinking, and basic feelings of self-worth. How does one go about directly teaching young people about cooperation? By examining the dictionary definition? Such discussion lacks reality and is too abstract. How does one make cooperation concrete? Put it in a bottle? Have students smell it, taste it, or touch it? Let them do some experiments with it?

There are two basic ways to develop concepts of abstract values. One is to create situations in the classroom in which students personally experience the values teachers desire to inculcate —thereby learning by doing. The other general way is to design experiences in which normal subject matter is integrated with value concepts.

Consider first a teaching technique that helps develop desirable values through actual experience. Traditionally schools have used the services of students in minor ways for visual aid squads, laboratory helpers, hall monitors, and school crossing guards. Teachers use monitors in the classroom for writing assignments on the board, checking attendance, and assorted clean-up duties. But such assistance is just the tip of the iceberg with regard to the full potential for student service. Junior and senior high school students could perform a very wide variety of functions. Some teenagers can be as effective with small children as adults. Young people could help coach children in physical activities, could organize clubs of all kinds, help with inventory and supplies, and participate in planning and conducting trips. It might add considerably to the reality—especially for students in poverty areas— if small but significant hourly payments were made for such work.

Evidence that a much greater share of responsibility for operating schools can be shouldered by students was offered by the Lower East Side Action Project (LEAP) in New York City, which enlisted dropouts to plan the curriculum, teach small groups, and even raise money for their own education. Students given such responsibilities usually reveal a high degree of awareness of what their real educational needs are and become more motivated to learn when their decisions and efforts begin to count. Similar planning responsibilities have been undertaken by even younger students as early as grade five in private institutions such as the Dalton School in New York City.

In one experiment in nineteen schools in New York City, each in a different school district and mainly with children from low socioeconomic areas, investigators from Brooklyn College found that a buddy system or classroom pairing approach to instructing students who were deficient in reading fostered many goals normally not achieved in schools. They state:

> The program provides a valuable mode for meeting pupils' individual needs, building values, and developing abilities. Expressed perceptions of feeling, accompanying the development of subject matter (in this case, reading) to some degree clarify children's thinking and understanding of how it feels to learn and to want to learn.
>
> The strong personal interactions and human relationships established between tutor and learner also exert a positive influence in making the educational process meaningful, and helps defuse the "joyless" aspects of traditional learning, particularly those of review and drill. All of these factors operate to produce a desire to learn and strong motivation, and thereby contribute to learning.
>
> The program provides opportunities to build in values that tend to be neglected in the customary school situation. Among the values that are positively strengthened are: self-respect, ego identity, self-image, satisfaction in achievement, social responsibility, sensitivity to others' needs, respect for others, satisfaction of the need to belong, human warmth and affection, freedom from fear and guilt concerning the pace of learning, and identification by the children with the teacher's problems.
>
> The program has a high degree of individualization with

respect to children's reading needs since each child is placed by the teacher at an instructional level suitable to his past achievement. Consequently, children who are at the lower levels of achievement are removed from the stressful situation of having to keep up with a too-rapid pace and are thereby involved in making more effective progress in a satisfying manner.

The constructive building of values and understandings, feelings of progress in learning and the high degree of individualized meeting of children's needs, all contribute to minimizing discipline problems. It was significant that none of the teachers reported any problems in this respect although many of the classes were in "difficult" schools, and the program purposely minimized direct teacher control over individual behavior. This suggests that the program has significant potential for stabilizing "difficult schools."[4]

One of the most effective ways of developing cooperative and democratic values is to organize small group activities, either for projects carried on as part of class work or outside on an extra-curricular basis. Anyone who has observed students participating in dramatic productions, athletic team events, debating competitions, exhibits at fairs, or fund-raising activities for teams or schools can readily identify the warm spirit, group unity, eagerness to cooperate and to share responsibilities within the group, and willingness to forego individual reward for group recognition and achievement.

Values are most successfully developed when students are given responsibilities for carrying out meaningful projects and are required to make important decisions. As an illustration, the following incident occurred between a group of college juniors preparing for teaching careers and four student members of the governing

---

[4] The complete report, *Classroom Pairing Tutorial Program* by Louise Mattioni and Belle Sharefkin, may be obtained at no cost from Book-Lab, Inc., 1449 37th St., Brooklyn, N.Y. 11218.

council of the previously mentioned LEAP school, which admits mainly high school dropouts. During a question period, the college students asked the LEAP students how they would deal with the use of marijuana by their fellow students. The LEAP students replied that a group decision about this very situation had been made recently. They had reasoned that if a student were caught smoking marijuana on school grounds, he would be jeopardizing the accreditation of the school and the education of other individuals; this consideration led the elected governing council to apply a penalty of expulsion. The college students insisted that such judgment by the council was too harsh and inconsistent with a humane type of school. The LEAP students were adamant in their position, stating that all students knew about the democratically decided-upon rule, and they insisted that in a democratic society the individual has to abide by important group decisions. They pointed out that at the same time the group must also accept responsibility for each member who will be ultimately making individual choices affecting the group. One may question whether all majority decisions must be forcefully imposed upon minorities, but at least these LEAP students had developed a strong value system, largely because of the responsibility they were encouraged to assume, the motivation to keep their school alive, and the experience of working together democratically.

The main point for educators is that a significant percentage of school time should be devoted to cooperative activities of this type, providing *real* experiences in which students learn-by-doing the values and skills that are now essentially absent from schooling. It does not follow that the traditional stress on competition be completely abandoned. Competition and cooperation are both important aspects of the real world, and it would be wrong to deprive students of adequate experience with either process. Today the experiences are unbalanced with competition overstressed and cooperation and democratic participation minimized. Specific attention to building cooperative values will redress the balance.

STUDENT-TEACHER INTERACTIONS

A teacher of ninth-grade science was describing the work of James Clark Maxwell who worked for years to develop an electromagnetic theory of light that ultimately led to discovery of radio waves and then to their application to modern television. A student interrupted with the surprising remark, "What a dope!" Pressed to explain, he replied, "He didn't get paid for it. Why did he do it?" The idea that a person would actually do difficult mental work for the benefit of mankind without any hope of deriving a fortune from it was totally alien to this young man and to some others in the class who agreed with him.

The teacher dropped the specific lesson for the day and devoted the remainder of the period to the questions raised by the student's remark. The outcome was a stimulating exchange of opinions among members of the class, with the teacher actively guiding the discussion with appropriate questions. In strong subject-centered schools, teachers must balance the worth of diversions that arise from students' remarks against the requirements of test-passing and marks and will probably have to limit such digressions to those that seem most likely to develop values. In a more reality-centered environment the number of such occasions may be expanded and the content broadened.

It is generally difficult for teachers of a class of thirty to know students as real human beings with likes and dislikes, personal and social problems, and attitudes and feelings that may obstruct the learning process. Rarely do they discover what really interests students, what their curiosities are, or the depth of their creative tendencies. However, some of these feelings, beliefs, and obstacles may be revealed in rap sessions in which students are allowed to discuss whatever problems trouble them or to make comments or raise questions of interest. Although the technique may seem more productive in an English or social studies class, some teachers have successfully used rap sessions in other subject areas.

The secret of success is to make students feel that regardless of what opinions or attitudes they express the teacher will insist on respect and consideration for differing ideas. If students feel that the teacher in any way attempts to impose his or her opinions and beliefs on them, then the rap session loses its value. This does not mean that the teacher should never give an opinion, only that it must be offered occasionally and on an equal basis with others—to be considered on its own merits and not as the authority of the teacher.

Of course, it would be unwise for a teacher to spend too much class time in such a manner, except in special situations where overwhelming psychological problems of students require it, as in a guidance class. Some teachers adopt a policy of devoting one period a week, or one every two weeks, to discussing whatever students wish to talk about, preferably related to the subject, but not in a hard and fast way. At the beginning, it may be necessary for the teacher to have on hand some general questions to initiate discussion, but once the ice has been broken, students will generally find enough to talk about on their own.

Careers and the world of jobs are of common interest in any subject, as are new developments and applicable newspaper and magazine accounts that fire the imagination. However, teachers should not hesitate to allow discussion of any topic close to the concerns of the students. In this respect the rap session may be considered a mild form of encounter session or group therapy, which can evoke many positive humanizing elements now missing from the educational process.

Another technique, which parallels the rap session, is to have students write a biographical sketch about themselves and to include anything they think will assist the teacher in understanding them. Frequently such a biographical sketch can provide valuable information about the interests and lives of students that can guide teachers in individualizing the course.

A variety of useful teaching techniques for developing value-related judgments are described in *Values Clarification: A Hand-*

book of Practice Strategies for Teachers and Students by Sidney Simon, Leland Howe, and Howard Kirschenbaum.[5] Reality-centered situations and questions involving values are presented, and different methods of evaluation are offered. Particularly suggestive for value-related activities are the numerous situations described, for example:

A blue-collar worker's son returns home from college for a holiday and criticizes his father for working for a company that is supplying war materials to Vietnam. The father becomes angry and points out that the money he earns in that plant is sending the son through college.

How do you feel about a college student selling pot in the local high school to pay for his tuition?

World War III breaks out and you are in charge of a bomb shelter that can only hold six people, but ten persons show up for admittance. They are: 1) a bookkeeper, 31 years old, 2) his wife, six months pregnant, 3) a black militant, a second-year medical student, 4) a famous historian and author, 42 years old, 5) a biochemist, 6) a rabbi, 54 years old, 7) an Olympic athlete, 8) a Hollywood starlet, singer, and dancer, 9) a college coed, and 10) a policeman with a gun. Which six do you allow into the shelter and why?

Dramatic situations such as these can be presented either to stimulate discussion or writing or as part of ongoing sessions exploring values.

An important element in exploring values is to involve students in developing strategies for sorting out and clarifying the values they encounter in real life. In this process parents, friends, peers, politicians, and heroes serve as models to identify with and emulate. In real life people first affirm and then act on beliefs they hold.

Values Clarification, cited above, provides teachers with numer-

---

[5] Published by Hart Publishing Co., 1972.

ous exercises for sorting out values and clarifying their meanings and effects. These include:

Values voting: Students indicate their likes, dislikes, and preferences for various values.

Rank order: One is required to make choices among many categories.

Value focus game: Emphasizes ways in which a small group interacts with an individual for mutual evaluation.

Risk ratio or forced field analysis: Helps students evaluate advantages and risks in determining the circumstances for affirming ideas, feelings, and actions.

Alternatives search: Testing and evaluating the action one can take.

Values in action: Thoughtful examination of choices and willingness to act on one's choices.

As a general illustration of the rank order technique, the following exercise might be presented in a social studies or science class:

Which item do you consider the most insurmountable problem man will face in the next century? Use 1 for the most insurmountable, 2 for the next most insurmountable, and so on.

World population control
Technology
Industrialization
War
Violence and crime in the streets
Control of disease
Food production

Such an exercise requires students to evaluate the importance of current social, political, economic, and scientific events and to extrapolate them into the future. The process requires them to think through not only how they view a given problem of modern life, but also the extent of their optimism or pessimism about the future solution of the problem.

MATERIALS FOR TEACHING VALUES

Direct experience with many kinds of values in school is often difficult to generate, so teachers must be alert to opportunities, be it an argument between students, the birth or death of a member of a student's family, or a personal problem that comes to light in a natural way and is suitable for class discussion. In most cases teachers will find it more feasible to design specific experiences around planned dramatizations or excerpts from newspapers, magazines, and books, or materials compiled for the purpose by teacher or students.

The key to reaching students is to provide situations that they recognize or accept as real, perhaps in the form of a dilemma or an open unanswered question presented in such a dramatic way that students are eager to pursue it. It is essential not to "answer" questions concerning values too readily, or even at all, because this inhibits the clash of opinions, which effectively produces thoughtful responses and possible changes.

Books and Stories

Many books about black history tell the story of Henry Brown, a southern slave who had a friend nail him into a crate just large enough to hold him in a cramped position; he was then shipped as freight to the North to freedom. A discussion of this incident would reveal the incredible hardships this escape entailed. Every student in the class can recognize that Henry Brown's act required extraordinary courage and must have been motivated by a burning desire to be a free man.

Judicious questions such as the following would readily elicit a dramatic discussion rich in value content: Try to imagine what it would be like to be shipped in a tight box for a trip lasting a week or more. What might have happened along the way? What happens if the heavy box is dropped, perhaps leaving the person inside with his head down and forced to remain that way (as actually occurred)? What would motivate a man to try to escape in this way? If you were a slave, would you lock yourself in a box to escape? Some people claim that the slaves in the South were happy and content with their lot. What do you think?

This incident will prompt a discussion that evokes deep understanding of what freedom must have meant to a slave, appreciation of the importance of freedom, feelings of sympathy for the plight of slaves, and an experience of empathy—seeing things from another person's view point. These feelings and concepts are closely interwoven with desirable values.

The following excerpt from Dick Gregory's autobiography *Nigger* is also sure to evoke an excellent discussion:

It was on a Thursday. I was sitting in the back of the room, in a seat with a chalk circle drawn around it. The idiot's seat, the troublemaker's seat.

The teacher thought I was stupid. Couldn't spell, couldn't read, couldn't do arithmetic. Just stupid. Teachers were never interested in finding out that you couldn't concentrate because you were so hungry, because you hadn't had any breakfast. All you could think about was noontime, would it ever come? Maybe you could sneak into the cloakroom and steal a bite of some kid's lunch out of a coat pocket. A bite of something. Paste. You can't really make a meal of paste, or put it on bread for a sandwich, but sometimes I'd scoop a few spoonfuls out of the big paste jar in the back of the room. Pregnant people get strange tastes. I was pregnant with poverty. Pregnant with dirt and pregnant with smells that made people turn away, pregnant with cold and pregnant with shoes that were never bought for me, pregnant with five other people in my bed and no Daddy in the next room, and pregnant with hunger. Paste doesn't taste too bad when you're hungry.

The teacher thought I was a troublemaker. All she saw from the front of the room was a little black boy who squirmed in his idiot's seat and made noises and poked the kids around him. I guess she couldn't see a kid who made noises because he wanted someone to know he was there.

It was on a Thursday, the day before the Negro payday. The eagle always flew on Friday. The teacher was asking each student how much his father would give to the Community Chest. On Friday night, each kid would get the money from his father, and on Monday he would bring it to the school. I decided I was going to buy me a Daddy right then. I had money in my pocket from shining shoes and selling papers, and whatever Helene Tucker pledged for her Daddy I was going to top it. And I'd hand the money right in. I wasn't going to wait until Monday to buy me a Daddy.

I was shaking, scared to death. The teacher opened her book and started calling out names alphabetically.

"Helene Tucker?"

"My Daddy said he'd give two dollars and fifty cents."

"That's very nice, Helene. Very, very nice indeed."

That made me feel pretty good. It wouldn't take too much to top that. I had almost three dollars in dimes and quarters in my pocket. I stuck my hand in my pocket and held onto the money, waiting for her to call my name. But the teacher closed her book after she called everybody else in the class.

I stood up and raised my hand.

"What is it now?"

"You forgot me."

She turned toward the blackboard. "I don't have time to be playing with you, Richard."

"My Daddy said he'd . . ."

"Sit down, Richard, you're disturbing the class."

"My Daddy said he'd give . . . fifteen dollars."

She turned around and looked mad. "We are collecting this money for you and your kind, Richard Gregory. If your Daddy can give fifteen dollars, you have no business being on relief."

"I got it right now, I got it right now, my Daddy gave it to me to turn in today, my Daddy said . . ."

"And furthermore," she said, looking right at me, her nostrils getting big and her lips getting thin and her eyes opening wide. "We know you don't have a Daddy."

Helene Tucker turned around, her eyes full of tears. She felt sorry for me. Then I couldn't see her too well because I was crying, too.

"Sit down, Richard."

And I always thought the teacher kind of liked me. She always picked me to wash the blackboard on Friday, after school. That was a big thrill, it made me feel important. If I didn't wash it, come Monday the school might not function right.

"Where are you going, Richard?"

I walked out of school that day, and for a long time I didn't go back very often. There was shame there.

Now there was shame everywhere. It seemed like the whole world had been inside that classroom, everyone had heard what the teacher had said, everyone had turned around and felt sorry for me. There was shame in going to the Worthy Boys Annual Christmas Dinner for you and your kind, because everybody knew what a worthy boy was. Why couldn't they just call it the Boys Annual Dinner, why'd they have to give it a name? There was shame in wearing the brown and orange and white plaid mackinaw the welfare gave to 3,000 boys. Why'd it have to be the same for everybody so when you walked down the street the people could see you were on relief? It was a nice warm mackinaw and it had a hood, and my Momma beat me and called me a little rat when she found out I stuffed it in the bottom of a pail full of garbage way over on Cottage Street. There was shame in running over to Mister Ben's at the end of the day and asking for his rotten peaches, there was shame in asking Mrs. Simmons for a spoonful of sugar, there was shame in running out to meet the relief truck. I hated that truck, full of food for you and your kind. I ran into the house and hid when it came. And then I started to sneak through alleys to take the long way home so the people going into White's Eat Shop wouldn't see me. Yeah, the whole world heard the teacher that day, we all know you don't have a Daddy.[6]

After this dramatic real-life passage is read by students, it will not require much prodding to get a discussion under way. Here are some appropriate questions: Dick Gregory is a comedian noted for his biting humor. How was it possible for his teacher to think of him as stupid? Have you ever been as hungry as Dick Gregory was? What does it feel like to be starving? How would you face the world if you had no father, were on welfare, and often went hungry? What connection does poverty have with ability to learn at school? Some white people think that blacks are less intelligent than whites. What do you think? Why did the teacher pass over Dick Gregory's name? Was she right in doing so? If you were that teacher, how would you have handled the situation? Have you ever been in a situation where you felt deeply ashamed because of something someone said or did to you?

Among the value-related concepts and attitudes encountered in such a discussion are: understanding of what it means to be poor and to have no father, how well-meaning people may unintentionally shame deprived people, why people seemingly act without thinking, and general empathy for people of other backgrounds. It is not necessary to formally state all the applicable values; often discussion of the experience carries its own message. However, there will be moments when teachers can highlight positive values with comments and additional experiences.

Reading magazine articles, short stories, or full-length novels in English and social studies classes can spark numerous value judgments. As an example, consider the *New York Times Magazine*

From *Nigger: An Autobiography* by Dick Gregory with Robert Lipsyte. New York: E. P. Dutton & Co., Inc., 1964.

for Sunday, June 30, 1974. "Decisions, Decisions, Decisions" by Lawrence Galton discusses the increasing likelihood that methods for predetermining the sex of children will soon be developed, and he presents some of the problems that might ensue. Will people prefer boys or girls and why? Would you prefer your children to be boys or girls? If people predominantly favor one sex, what social outcomes follow? How will this affect the lives of men and women? A discussion around these questions probes deeply held values concerning basic human relationships.

"SALT in a MAD World" by Jack Ruina discusses the balance of nuclear armed might or "mutual assumed destruction" (MAD) by which the United States and the Soviet Union keep each other at arm's length and precariously refrain from going too far and provoking a nuclear war. A full-page cartoon shows Nixon and Brezhnev embracing each other, with grossly stretched jackets from which enormous quantities of nuclear missiles protrude. The article raises many questions involving attitudes toward peace and war, "enemies," "one world or none," and pessimism or optimism about the future of the world.

A third article, "Spirit of '74" by Thomas Fleming, suggests 1774 as a more appropriate date for the beginning of the American Revolution and details the fascinating events in England and America that led to revolution and civil war. The classic confrontation of the oppressor and the oppressed and the customary blindness of autocrats and masters to the reactions of those they seek to control are vividly described and raise many questions about more modern events and even personal disputes.

"Ed Who?" discusses the decreasing interest in space flight. "Ed Who" is Edward Gibson, the scientist astronaut who was one of the three-man team that circled the globe in Skylab in 1973 for a record eighty-four days. The article asks, "How do you explain the fact that more Americans know who Alice Cooper is than who this man is?" Discussion of the article can reveal a great deal about attitudes toward new events, evaluation of the significance f an event, and rapid acceptance by people of today's many ighly unusual and important happenings as commonplace.

Finally, a satiric piece, "Homage to George" by Russell Baker, suggests to modern Americans that they are honoring the wrong George. Baker develops a proposal that the forthcoming bicentennial celebration of 1776 should focus on King George III and not George Washington. He recounts similarities of America's power in the world today with that of England in 1776 and compares the basic attitudes of the English in 1776 with those of Americans today. Many value-related attitudes of students would be aroused in discussing this article.

All five major articles in this one magazine could be sources for value-oriented discussions. There is no dearth of material—all a teacher need do is to select content of suitable reading level and appropriate interest.

News Clippings

News clippings can also help develop value concepts. For instance, if a social phenomenon familiar to students takes place in another country, they are able to see the human relationships more objectively and can more easily reveal their own deep feelings and prejudices. The following November 11, 1973 news story provides insight into the universal problem of social antagonisms and the conditions that cause them.

Marseilles And Arabs Are Uneasy
by Oliver G. Howard

MARSEILLES, France—Unease, apprehension and suspicion are still apparent among the Arabs in their section of Marseilles despite a gradual easing of the racial tensions and the virtual disappearance of the violence that followed the murder of a bus conductor here on Aug. 25 by a deranged Algerian.

This violence saw Arabs attacked and beaten and eleven of

them killed, some as far away as Metz and Paris, almost five hundred miles from this Mediterranean port city.

Some French in Marseilles say this violence was an isolated flare-up, resulting from a combination of circumstances unlikely to occur again. They also say that the events here were fed by false rumor that a dozen people were killed when an Algerian, Salah Bougrine, thirty-eight years old, ran amok with a kitchen knife, and that gangs of Arabs were attacking buses and Europeans.

Most Are Pessimistic

But a majority of the French here who gave their views are more pessimistic. With nearly a million North Africans working in France, they say, there is no possibility of assimilation, and racial violence is likely to erupt again when circumstances make the moment ripe. They feel that only a concerted effort on the part of national and local leaders and religious and social organizations can reduce this likelihood.

A minority of Frenchmen here take a more primitive view. When they speak of North Africans they make clear that they mean Algerians. The Tunisians and Moroccans in France number only about 250,000, are generally better educated and have skills that enable them to hold white-collar jobs. The North Africans, these Frenchmen say, have no moral sense, understand nothing but force and must be kept in their place.

Here in Marseilles their place is the Arab quarter, just north of La Canebrière, the city's most elegant avenue.

Its narrow streets are lined with dingy shops and decrepit-looking hotels, mostly run by French who live outside the quarter. There are also many Arab bars and a few restaurants. The most striking feature is the almost total lack of women and children, for most of the Arabs have left their families in Algeria. . . .

The common complaint among the Arabs is that they are being harried by the police, especially in the last two months, having to produce their identity papers and work permits on the slightest pretext, or none at all. They said they were pushed, shoved and elbowed by Frenchmen in the streets and shops outside the Arab section. If an Arab shoves back, they said, he will probably be beaten, and when the police come he will be arrested and jailed.

Aside from the fear of physical violence, the Arabs also spoke with some bitterness of their inability to get any but the lowest paid and most unskilled jobs—jobs they said Frenchmen would not accept—and of not being given training and experience to permit them to move to higher-paying jobs.

They cannot get decent housing, they said, and are overcharged for what they can get. . . .[7]

Some typical questions about this news item might be: How is the situation described similar to problems in the United States? What are the main reasons for French antagonisms toward the Algerians? Why are Algerians hostile to the French? How do educational inequality, poverty, and poor living conditions contribute to social conflict? If you were a Frenchman interested in solving problems of social conflict, what kind of program would you work for?

Similar news items about the civil wars between Catholics and Protestants in Northern Ireland and between Hindus and Moslems in India as well as perennial clashes among other groups appear frequently, and a collection of such clippings can provide material for an excellent reality-centered unit on race relations.

If teachers do not have at hand a news clipping suitable for a specific value to be discussed, they—or students—can compose a simulated news story, as in the following example:

August 13, X-ville—John Parker, a forty-five-year-old automobile mechanic waiting for a bus on State Street and Polk

---

Avenue, was mugged by two young men who robbed him of
his wallet containing $45 and fled through an alleyway after
punching him and knocking him to the ground.

Police were given descriptions of the attackers by by-
standers.

Mr. Parker complained to the reporters that he received no
assistance from the many people on the street. "There must
have been a dozen able-bodied men nearby who did abso-
lutely nothing while I called for help. If even three or four
had come to my rescue, we could easily have captured them,
or at least driven them off. I don't know what's wrong with
people that they won't stick together in the face of a common
danger."

Such a simulated story can initiate an animated discussion
about personal involvement, helping other people, personal sacri
fice, and the dangers of city life.

Educational Publications

Materials dealing with value-related personal decisions are be
ginning to be issued by educational publishers. For example, her
is a letter describing a situation for class discussion:

Dear Ellie:

I am in a class for kids who need extra help. When I walk
down the halls, other kids laugh and call me "special." They
say I am different and joke about the way I look. I can't stand
this hurt anymore, but I want to get an education. I need
your advice.

P.T., Minnesota[8]

A situation such as this, which is presented as a problem fo
someone else, makes it possible for students to view it less emo

---

[8] Available in the unit "Youth Generation," published by Scholastic Boo
Services, Englewood Cliffs, N.J. 07632.

tionally than if it were their own and widens the scope of a value-based discussion.

Standard textbooks and supplementary source materials often contain useful excerpts for teaching values. Here is an extract from a test booklet that can serve this function:

> Some customs of the Japanese seem strange to us. And some of our ways appear strange to them.
>
> We sleep on soft pillows and beds; they sleep on hard ones. We wash our faces and wipe them dry with dry towels; they wipe their faces with wet towels. We lower our faces when we say grace; they raise theirs. When entering houses our men take off their hats; the Japanese take off their shoes. We give gifts when arriving; they leave them when departing. We open gifts in front of the giver; they never do. When in mourning, we wear black; they wear white. We frown when scolded; they smile.
>
> When we say that Japanese, Chinese, Indians, and other Asiatics are strange people, they could reply, "The same to you."[9]

This brief account can motivate a discussion of the cultural variations students can observe in their own community. If there are foreign-born students in the class, they can be encouraged to describe their reactions to the strange customs of the United States. Students who have been abroad can recount their observations of strange customs in other lands. The concepts of strangeness and stranger may then be related to the shallow basis for our likes, dislikes, and prejudices.

Poetry and Music

Language differences can stimulate similar discussions of cultural differences, as suggested in the following poem:

---

[9] William A. McCall and Lelah Mae Crabbs. *Standard Test Lessons in Reading*, Book A. New York: Teachers College Press, 1961.

We Say—They Say
Flo Gozlin

Expressions that are natural for us
   in the U.S.A.
Are said by English people in quite
   a different way.

For instance, we "take a vacation,"
   but they "go on a holiday."
We do many things "at once" while
   they do them "straightway."

Our alphabet's final letter is Z, but the
   English called it zed.
In school, we "have a recess"; they
   "take a break" instead.

A statement we close with a period;
   the English use a "full stop."
They call a policeman a "bobby,"
   while we call ours a "cop."

We talk about "walking a block"; they
   go "to the top of the street."
A piece of "hard candy" here, in England is called a "boiled sweet."

In their country, a "chesty" person is
   suffering from a cold;
Their "nervy" person is nervous, never
   presumptuous or bold.

Our "mail box" they call their "pillar
   box," and our "mail" would be their
   "post."
Their "joint of beef" would be to us
   "a piece of good beef roast."

> The English "tune in on the wireless"
> while we "listen to the radio."
> They're saying "good-by" in a pleasant
> way when they call out, "Cheerio!"

The lyrics and music for songs often offer thoughts and suggest emotions that can stimulate value-related discussions. For example, the simple, haunting melody and poignant words of "The Strangest Dream" by Ed McCurdy offer students who have never experienced the horrors of war a glimpse into what such an experience might have been and why "peace on earth" has always been a hope of mankind.

Popular songs such as "The Impossible Dream" by Joe Darin and Mitch Leigh and "Eleanor Rigby" by John Lennon are representative of those that evoke emotional imagery and have potential for value-related discussions.

Visual Materials

Many newspaper photographs can stimulate discussions concerning values. For instance, look at the photograph of Prime Minister Bhutto of Pakistan and Prime Minister Sheik Mujibur Rahman of Bangladesh embracing like long lost brothers in June 1974, three years after a revolution and civil war in which Bangladesh (formerly East Pakistan) won its independence from West Pakistan. Hundreds of thousands of people were killed in the struggle, many atrocities were committed, and hatred ran deep. No one would have thought it possible that only three years later representatives of such bitter enemies would be embracing in public.

This photograph and the circumstances in which it was taken could start a discussion about enmity. When the people of one nation hate those of another, generally as the result of war or conquest, will they always do so? Despite one hundred years of hostility, do the French and Germans now hate each other? In the

early 1950s the Russians and Chinese were apparently great
friends, but now they seem to be bitter enemies. During World
War II Germans were equated with Nazis by most Americans, and
the Japanese were considered wily, untrustworthy, hateful men.
Now we are good friends of the Germans and Japanese. President
Nixon gained political support for his vigorously anti-Communist,
anti-Russian, and anti-Chinese positions, but when he became

president, he established personal friendships with the leaders of his former enemies, and they reciprocated.

Such examples can lead to a consideration of current conflicts. At the time of this writing it seems inconceivable that the Israelis and the Arabs, particularly the Palestinian refugees, will ever sit down together and cooperate, but one should not be surprised if some time in the future they overcome their animosities. Perhaps the Catholics and Protestants in Northern Ireland will one day overcome hundreds of years of hatred and live together amicably. And what about hatreds within our own nation? What groups in the United States dislike or hate each other and why? How can such aversions be overcome? The discussion can be extended to personal relationships. Why do people dislike each other as individuals? Examples can be elicited from personal experiences.

A file of photographs clipped from newspapers and magazines can motivate many lessons involving values. Perhaps the audio-visual or media department can convert them into slides so that they could be magnified on a screen for class viewing.

Films also offer much realistic material to initiate discussions about values. One specially designed five-minute film of this nature opens with a scene of a teenage girl washing dishes.[10] Her mother, about to leave the house, warns the girl that she is to mind the baby, do her homework, and not to let her boyfriend visit that evening. After the mother leaves, the boyfriend appears and persuades the girl to go with him to the corner drugstore for a soda. On the way the girl witnesses a fatal hit-and-run accident and is alert enough to observe the license plate number of the car. Shortly afterwards she is approached by a policeman who asks if she saw anything that would help them find the driver. The image of the license plate number flashes onto the screen, and the film ends with the implied question, "Would you get involved by telling the police the license plate number and then probably be punished

---

[10] *It's Your Move*. New Dimensions in Education, 160 DuPont St., Plainview, N.Y. 11803.

by your mother when she inevitably found out that you disobeyed her?"

This brief film motivates discussion of important values without preaching. [If a school is organized by subject areas, teachers could slant the lesson toward the objectives of specific subjects— an English teacher toward writing a composition and oral discussion skills, and a social studies teacher toward social problems.]

Excerpts from full-length feature films, which offer realistic material for value discussions, are available. For example, in a twenty-eight-minute excerpt from A Man for All Seasons, entitled "Conscience In Conflict,"[11] Sir Thomas Moore, Lord Chancellor of England and friend of King Henry the Eighth, struggles with his conscience and loyalties. Should he do what he believes to be right and oppose the king's efforts to divorce his wife and marry Anne Boleyn, thereby invoking the king's wrath and possibly risking execution, or should he take the much more prudent course and maintain his power, prestige, wealth, and life? There are many parallels to his situation today, for example, Watergate, Vietnam War protesters, and the Eichmann trial.

Another film available from the same source, "Whether to Tell the Truth," is a fifteen-minute excerpt from On the Waterfront. Marlon Brando portrays a young dock worker who slowly realizes that he can no longer remain silent about the corruption and gangster killings he observes and comes to feel that he must tell the crime commission what he knows, even though this means grave personal danger. This will provoke consideration of current problems of fighting crime at the expense of personal risks and the broader problems of involvement in social issues.

Other short films[12] prompt students to explore options, think about alternatives, and consider the results of their decisions. For example, Those Who Mourn presents the problems of accepting

---

[11] Learning Corporation of America, 711 Fifth Ave., New York, N.Y. 10022. Also see its Film Utilization Catalogue, Special Edition, 1974.
[12] TeleKETICS, 1229 South Santee St., Los Angeles, Calif. 90015. A complete catalog is available on request.

death and *Let The Rain Settle It* deals with racial understanding.

Even comic strips can spark lessons concerning values.[13] For example, the following strip presented enlarged on a screen with an overhead projector can challenge a class to relate the incident to human relationships. Some responses might be: "People sometimes prefer the old and familiar to the new and strange," "Is it always progress when something new and shiny replaces something old and worn?" "Good deeds are not always appreciated,"

LIFE WITH LUCKY

NATIONAL ENQUIRER, LANTANA, FLA. USED BY PERMISSION.

[13] Leonard Kenworthy. *Background Papers for Social Studies Teachers.* Belmont, Calif.: Wadsworth Publishing Co., 1966.

or "Does the doer of a deed always know or care about what the recipient wants?"

Similar rich sources for value studies may be found in TV scenes, especially commercials familiar to students. For example, a commercial for small cigars (replacing cigarette ads that are now banned on TV) shows a young man and his girl friend strolling through the grass and then sitting down to rest as he lights up his "cougherillo." The girl watches adoringly as the smoke curls around his face and hers. The amorality of a commercial that promotes an unhealthy product by making it seem attractive, manly, and sexually appealing will be readily apparent to students.

Another commercial shows a happy man who announces to his wife that their financial worries are over. He has just come from a finance company that has assumed all his burdensome debts, lent him money to go on a vacation to Hawaii, and postponed payments for not so far into the future. There is not a hint of a suggestion that the debt will have to be paid back later with high interest. This commercial could be related to the well-known fable of the grasshopper and the ant.

Mimeographed sheets containing the verbatim scripts of commercials, accompanied by suitable questions, can be prepared. Students can watch their own favorite commercials and analyze them for both value and consumer content. Such activities, which relate to the real world and encourage individual initiative and creativity, are educationally valuable and very motivating as well.

REALITY 𝕊
AND THE 𝕊
"BIG IDEA" 𝕊

𝕊 The point was made earlier that traditional education neglects many big ideas that are essential to understanding today's realities, mainly because of the artificial nature of traditional subjects. The classroom teacher must somehow bridge the gap between the rigid limitations of subject and the big ideas that enable one to grasp difficult realities and relationships in the outside world. Consider some of the major problems of our time—a population explosion, pollution, energy crises, and, inflation. To understand these problems, students must comprehend the nature of growth, which requires an understanding of the mathematics of growth.

NATURE OF GROWTH

The mathematics of growth is closely related to geometric progression, normally taught in upper level algebra courses. Mathematics teachers are generally more interested in algebraic relationships for geometric progressions than in their application, and it is unlikely that their students will connect the real problems of population or economic growth with what is learned in class, except in a superficial way. Further, students will probably not do an in-depth analysis of the nature of growth in social studies or economics classes where teachers may not feel competent to teach the mathematics involved or believe that it is inappropriate to do so. Some students will never study upper level math or economics and will completely miss any discussion of the vital subject of growth.

Growth can easily be discussed in depth in a unit in mathematics, social studies, or English in grades seven to ten if teachers adopt a reality-centered approach emphasizing what students need to know. The mathematics required to understand growth may be treated in a totally nonalgebraic way using tools most students possess.

The extent to which teachers make use of the following mathematical relationships depends largely on their subject specialties and situations. A social studies teacher would probably not have time to go into the kind of detail described here, while a mathematics teacher would, and a science teacher might. Of course, if the unit is a study of growth, no problem arises. Teachers who do not wish to pursue the mathematical detail could merely present the relationships, without proof, or have groups of mathematically talented students work out the details and present them to the class.

A unit on growth might begin with a discussion of population explosions, a topic that will interest most students. To make the subject real, pose the problem of calculating how the population of a town grows if it begins with 100 people and increases by 10 percent a year. The 10 percent rate, although unusually large, offers the substantial advantage of easy calculation for the annual increase by simply moving the decimal point one place to the left. The population growth may then be shown if students construct a table of the kind shown on the opposite page.

Table I: Ten Percent
Annual Growth Rate

A	B	C	D
Year	Population at Beginning of Year	Amount of Increase During Year (1/10 x B)	Population at End of Year
Start	100 ←(1)	10	110
1	110	11	121
2	121	12.1	133.1
3	133.1	13.3	146.4
4	146.4	14.6	161.0
5	161.0	16.1	177.1
6	177.1	17.7	194.8
7	194.8 ←(2)	19.5	214.3
8	214.3	21.4	235.7
9	235.7	23.6	259.3
10	259.3	25.9	285.2
11	285.2 ←(3)	28.5	313.7
12	313.7	31.4	345.1
13	345.1	34.5	379.6
14	379.6 ←(4)	38.0	417.6
15	417.6	41.8	459.4
16	459.4	45.9	505.3
17	505.3 ←(5)	50.5	555.8
18	555.8	55.6	611.4
19	611.4 ←(6)	61.1	672.5
20	672.5 ←(7)	67.3	739.8
21	739.8	74.0	813.8
22	813.8 ←(8)	81.4	895.2
23	895.2 ←(9)	89.5	984.7
24	984.7 ←(10)	98.5	1083.2
25	1083.2 ←(11)	108.3	1191.5

Observe that the population increase (column C) grows at an ever-increasing pace. Whereas the population increase the first year is 10, by the end of the eighth year it is more than twice as large or 21.4. By the end of the twelfth year, only four years later, the increase is more than three times as large, 31.4, as the original 10. By the end of the twenty-fifth year the annual increase is 108.3, more than ten times as large as the first year. As they perform the calculation for each year or study the table, students may also observe that the amount of annual increase grows at an increasing pace. For the first year 10 percent is taken of 100, while at the tenth year 10 percent is taken of 259.3, and at the 25th year the increase is 10 percent of 1083.2.

Some idea of the rapid increase in population may be obtained from column B where the numbers in the parentheses indicate when the population increases by increments of 100. The first increase of 100 occurs during the seventh year, but the next increase of 100 occurs only four years later. Students may observe that by the twenty-fourth year a population increase of 100 occurs every year.

Another facet of the nature of growth at a constant rate may be observed from the time required for population to double. It takes a bit more than seven years for the first doubling to 200; another seven plus years for the second doubling to about 400; another seven plus years to double again to 800.

In a more advanced group graphic analysis can contribute considerably to understanding the nature of population growth. As students plot a graph of column B of Table I, they will observe how the steepness of the curve constantly increases. The nature of the doubling process may also be shown graphically with the dotted lines at the 200, 400, and 800 population marks, all of which occur at constant increments of slightly more than seven years.

The graph also proves useful for quickly answering a number of questions. "When will the population reach 350, or 640, or 1075?" "What will the population be after 4.6 years, or 9.4 years, or 20 years and 3 months?"

The property of doubling in equal periods of time is characteristic of all growth situations where the rate of growth is constant. The time for doubling population is seven plus years for a 10 percent growth rate, a 5 percent growth rate has a doubling period of 14 plus years, a 2 percent growth rate produces doubling every 35 plus years, and a 1 percent growth rate causes doubling every 70 years. These figures may be easily verified with an electronic calculator, especially the kind that has a button for a constant (K), which in this case represents the annual multiplier. Figures

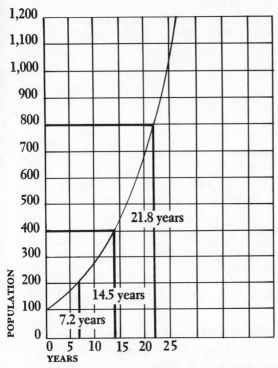

such as those in Table I could be generated with a calculator for any percentage of growth in a minute or so. Such tables and accompanying graphs could be produced by more capable students as special projects.

Doubling in equal time periods permits a simple, non-algebraic method of estimating population growth over long periods of time. A population that doubles ten times will increase about 1,000 times, which may be expressed as $1 \times 2 \times 2 \times 2 \times 2 \times 2 \times 2 \times 2 \times 2 \times 2 \times 2$. This equals 1,024, which is approximately 1,000. The teacher may pose a realistic problem by asking students to figure out what the 200,000,000 population of the United States in 1970 will be in the future if it doubles every thirty years, a rate characteristic of the pre-1970 period. Ten doublings would occur in 10 × 30 years or 300 years, and the population would grow about 1,000 times

Table II: Population Growth of the United States
(Assuming Population Doubles Every 30 Years)

Year	Population
1970	200 million 200,000,000, or 2×10^8*
2000	400 million 400,000,000, or 4×10^8
2300	1,000 × 400 million, or 400,000 million, or 400 billion 400,000,000,000, or 4×10^{11}
2600	1,000 × 400 billion, or 400,000 billion, or 400 trillion 400,000,000,000,000, or 4×10^{14}
2900	1,000 × 400 trillion, or 400,000 trillion, or 400 quadrillion 400,000,000,000,000,000, or 4×10^{17}

* (10^8 represents 2 followed by 8 zeros)

every 300 years. Students can now construct a new table such as Table II.

The larger the population becomes, the more it grows, hence these astoundingly large figures. The numbers—purely mathematical abstractions—clearly reveal why man must control population increases. The point may be further emphasized by calculating population densities (number of persons per unit of land area). The teacher may supply the information (or have students look it up in the library) that the land area of the United States is about three and one half million square miles. With this fact and the figures in Table II students may calculate that by the year 2900, if growth doubles every thirty years, there would be an average of 100 billion people per square mile, vastly greater than the current entire population of the United States! If some enterprising student calculates the concentration per square foot, he will discover that every square foot area would have to accommodate 4,000 people! It takes no special imagination to realize that such a situation is impossible.

If students pursue the matter for a slower rate of growth, say 1 percent annually with a doubling period of 70 years, they will discover that the situation would be similar, except that it would take a longer time to reach an equivalent population.

The explosive nature of growth at a constant rate may also be driven home with several dramatic illustrations of the consequences of doubling a quantity. Pose the problem of estimating the thickness of a wad of newspaper that has been folded in half 100 times, assuming a paper thickness of 3 thousandths of an inch. As noted previously, the first 10 doublings would produce a thickness 1000 times the original thickness. Thereafter every 10 foldings multiply the thickness another 1000 times. Multiplication by 1000 would occur ten times in 100 foldings. The final thicknesses of paper would be about 1000 multiplied by itself 10 times over or 1,000,000,000,000,000,000,000,000,000,000 (10^{30}). Even if the paper is only .003 inches thick, this number represents an enormous thickness, much larger than the distance to the farthest known galaxy in the universe, ten billion light years away!

For another direct growth situation students might calculate the germ population when one germ doubles by means of fission in an hour, then doubles repeatedly to 4, to 8, to 16, and so on for twenty days. Students may use a method of estimating based on the fact that ten doublings multiply a quantity by about 1,000. The final number may be estimated as follows:

1. In 20 days there are 20 × 24 hours, or 480 hours. Therefore the germs will double in number 480 times.

2. 480 doublings is the same as 48 × 10 doublings, and 10 doublings produces a multiplication of about 1,000 times. Therefore, 480 doublings is the same as 1,000 multiplied by itself 48 times. When the students multiply these 48 groups of 1,000 they obtain the number: 1,000,000,000,000,000,000,000,000,000,000,000,-000,000,000,000,000,000,000,000,000,000,000,000,000,000,000,-000,000,000,000,000,000,000,000,000,000,000,000,000,000,000,-000,000,000,000,000. This enormous number may be stated more simply as 10^{144}. It is so vast that the volume of such a quantity of germs would be quadrillions of times greater than that of the

entire known universe! Obviously, germs could never reach such a quantity.

Advanced students in a math class could be asked to calculate how long it would take the germs to fill the school building (assuming constant rate of growth and solid packing of germs), or the earth, sun, solar system, or entire universe (using the formula for volume of a sphere: $V = \frac{4}{3} \pi R^3$). Such calculations lead students to understand why, sooner or later, a zero rate of population growth must be achieved. They can readily see that if population growth is not limited, the earth's finite resources will inevitably be overtaxed and man's growth will cause shortages of food, increased illnesses, perhaps wars over resources, and higher death rates.

The real nature of growth has immediate applications to the energy crisis, to outmoded concepts of progress as a constantly growing Gross National Product, (G.N.P.), to the necessity to husband resources, and to rejection of economies based solely on satisfying constantly increasing, unlimited consumer demands, many of which are not essential. Basic concepts in economics are involved in revising G.N.P. as a measure of progress and substituting some kind of Gross National Use (G.N.U.) index that expresses the usefulness of what is produced and consumed.

Mathematical projections may be made for pollution problems, based on constant growth in car use and similar energy-consuming devices. This kind of analysis could also demonstrate the ultimate folly of wars, with their expenditures of vast quantities of increasingly scarce resources—oil, metals, chemicals, and natural products.

Even nuclear explosions may be brought into the picture by studying the nature of a chain reaction. The process of increasing the numbers of exploding nuclei is similar to the growth of any population, but in this case the doubling period is extremely short, in fact, less than a millionth of a second. The "population" of exploding nuclei can be figured with essentially the same arithmetic calculations used for human population.

Note how this reality-oriented approach takes mathematics out of the dull "What is this good for?" category and puts it right up on the front page of the newspaper. The "big ideas" that emerge from a mathematical study of growth become integrated with economics, science, current events, and good citizenship. What more can one ask of a subject that now produces mental blocks in so many students? How many students would be more motivated to seek learning of this kind?

Note, too, that this reality-centered "big idea" can be introduced before students learn about geometric progression in upper level algebra classes. If the reality of the "big idea" comes first, then the mathematical techniques automatically flow out of it. Students perform in a motivated framework in which math is a powerful tool for understanding the world. At the same time they obtain practice in calculating with percentages, constructing tables, learning about exponents, making graphs, and preparing a solid conceptual base for understanding the algebra of geometric progressions later. By the time they reach the algebra class, they will know why mathematics is useful and won't have to question its value, as many do.

CHALLENGING ACCEPTED IDEAS

Anyone who has ever challenged a deeply held majority belief, opinion, or "fact" has learned the hard way how many otherwise reasonable minds are tightly closed in some important respects, generally with strong emotional overtones. Yet solving human problems often involves challenging accepted ideas and finding new paths. It is important to provide young people with experiences in which they can learn to tolerate the viewpoints of others who hold different beliefs, opinions, and even "facts." Unfortunately, many such situations involve controversial issues about which students already have strong opinions. It is essential to develop classroom situations that involve seeing other points of view in noncontroversial and nonemotional contexts.

As an example, a teacher (or a student or group of students) could assume the role of a person who has just been transported by a time machine to the twentieth century from the year 1400 A.D. and who argues with the class about the currently accepted thesis that the earth is round. The citizen of 1400 asks the class to, "Prove to me that the earth is round and that it rotates daily and revolves around the sun." Invariably students—even at the college level—proceed with great confidence, having "learned" the subject quite well in earlier years. Even a decade after earth satellites have sent back photographs of a round earth, taken from outer space, students often present as the first piece of evidence the fact that when a sailboat moves away from shore toward the horizon, one sees only the sail at the top of the boat and not the lower part of the vessel. "Did you ever see that?" produces an astonished look, as though it were irrelevant. Occasionally a student will claim that he has seen this phenomenon, but most never have. Their facts are completely divorced from their personal reality.

"But," continues the time-transported citizen, "with my own eyes I saw the sun rise in the east this morning. And last night I saw it move downward in the west. I feel with my body that the earth is perfectly still and does not move. You tell me about evidence gathered by other people, far away. I prefer to believe my senses."

In the ensuing discussion the number of startling assumptions students have made about the round earth and its motions becomes apparent. Although they have been told that the surface of the earth moves about 1,000 miles an hour as it revolves on its axis, few have really wondered why they do not feel the motion in the slightest degree. When gravity is introduced to explain why people don't fall off the earth in Australia, the citizen from 1400 A.D. asks, "Who is he?" In the attempt to explain, the fantastic properties of the force of gravity become literally astounding. It is a mysterious force, very much like an ancient genie or spirit, that pulls everything toward the earth, without strings, or ropes, or chains, or any material connection.

The 1400 A.D. visitor is not convinced. "Nothing stops it or alters it—even if I put a ten-foot stone block between me and the earth! You mean to tell me that this spirit even pulls the moon at a distance of a quarter million miles and keeps it on course? Are you really serious about your claim that the moon pulls the earth's water away from the solid earth and creates the tides?"

This recital of impossibles makes it clear to all that the students have not thought much about gravity, or even questioned it, and do not understand the difficulties of proving that the earth is a round, rotating, revolving planet, or the reasons why this seemed so outlandish to even highly intelligent people in ancient times. What opportunities for *real* teaching in depth have been missed!

What is wrong, of course, is the way these concepts have been taught—superficially, with little or no relationship to reality and historical perspective and with no respect for the inherent, very real contradictions to our senses.

INTERRELATEDNESS OF MODERN LIFE

In former times, when transportation and communication were limited, important events or human decisions that occurred in one town or village had little or no effect on people in other parts of the region or nation or on other nations. But today, with vastly improved transportation and communication, an event or decision made in one place will often have worldwide repercussions in a short time. Webs of social, political, and economic relationships are national in extent, and often global. A pull, a tug, a tear, or a change in that web in one place can affect the fabric elsewhere.

An attempt to repair a web, or reform it, or change it often produces effects that are difficult to foresee or anticipate. Frequently, a socioeconomic invention intended to bring about reform may be so superficially designed or so defective in concept that it boomerangs and creates new economic, political, or social problems as difficult to solve as the original ones or even more so. During a period of rapid change, the evolving social structure may be so altered that an originally effective socioeconomic invention may have unintended, adverse effects.

It is important to devote some time in the social studies curriculum to studying this phenomenon of interrelationships and to letting students apply the concept to specific current problems. The following list of interrelationships should suffice to explore the general nature of the concept; each could be expanded into a research project.

1. Use of a new tranquilizer in Europe caused price increases for many new drugs in the United States.

   Thalidomide became very popular in Europe and was frequently prescribed by doctors. About the same time a sharp increase in the number of unusual deformities in newborn babies was noted. By means of ingenious research, the cause of the birth defects was traced to the taking of Thalidomide by pregnant women. As a consequence of this discovery, procedures for testing and approving new drugs were made more stringent in the United States, and the development of new drugs is now more time-consuming and costly. Ultimately this extra cost is reflected in the selling price of the drug.

2. Social Security regulations, originally designed to increase employment and to make retirement possible for older people, can have the effect of impoverishing large numbers of the elderly.

   During the Depression jobs for able-bodied men were scarce, and to increase the number of jobs the Social Security laws included income limitations. Elderly people were encouraged to retire and live on their Social Security payments, but if they worked and earned more than a certain small amount per year, their payments were reduced or stopped. During the Depression years this system worked, and many elderly persons retired, opening up jobs for younger people.

Today, with higher standards of living, the income limitations are so strict that many older people do not retire and continue to work. Some who do retire, find their Social Security incomes inadequate and at the poverty level. They are locked into ever-decreasing real income by inflation. In addition, various legal inequities have developed. For example, if an individual receives a million dollars a year from interest and dividends, he or she may receive full Social Security benefits, but if a person works for wages above a certain amount, his or her Social Security benefits are withheld. All institutional structures evolve and require periodic reform to keep them effective.

3. Improved technology for drilling oil wells, developed largely in the United States, helped make distant, small, underdeveloped countries the most prosperous on earth.

Improved technology for drilling oil wells during the first half of the twentieth century lowered the cost of fuel oil and gasoline to a level where demand rose at an explosive rate. As a result oil companies from the United States, Great Britain, and other industrialized countries sought oil everywhere on earth. Vast oil reserves were found in Mideast countries such as Kuwait, Iran, and Saudi Arabia, which were then undeveloped and impoverished desert lands. Today they have the highest per capita income on earth and are rapidly becoming the richest nations with vast economic power over other nations and the global economy.

4. Improved health care in industrial nations has contributed to food shortages in the poor countries of Africa and Asia.

Missionaries and medical teams from the United States and other industrial nations applied their medical techniques to improve health care in undeveloped nations. Death rates dropped dramatically, but little or no attention was paid to curbing birth rates, and the populations increased rapidly. Soon the available food supply was overtaxed, leading to malnutrition, starvation, and death in many areas. It is not easy to curb birth rates because of deep-seated cultural, religious, and social patterns.

5. Increased use of technology in the fishing industry has raised the cost of fish, an effect that would not have been anticipated by the classical concept of technological improvements.

   Technological know-how such as radar, sonar, more efficient ships, and the like have been utilized by Japan and the Soviet Union in the construction of modern fishing vessels that can quickly find schools of fish and whales and process catches directly on board ship. Fishing was pursued so intensively that many species were rapidly decimated and became more difficult to find and catch. The resulting scarcity of fish and whale products increased the price of fish considerably. Further, the cost of these vessels was so large that fishing has been intensified to prevent losses of the investments, and it will be difficult to stop the overfishing before entire species of sea life are completely wiped out.

   This problem is complicated with interrelationships, many of which involve international law. Who owns the sea? How far out into the ocean do the borders of a country extend? Does a landlocked nation have any rights to products from the sea? It is worthwhile for students to pursue such questions in detail because of their many ramifications in different areas.

6. The automobile has made people less neighborly and concerned about each other.

   Before the automobile, the neighborhood was the major center of life for most people. Most social life took place within a moderate walking distance of one's home. But where cars are available, one's friends may be scattered over a fifty-mile radius, and people have less time for their neighbors and less interest in them as people.

7. Widespread construction of nuclear power plants may weaken the defense potential of an industrial nation.

   An ordinary dynamite-type bomb or a very small nuclear

bomb dropped on a nuclear power station would release enormous amounts of radiation into the air, potentially killing large numbers of people and making large areas uninhabitable. Construction of numerous nuclear power plants renders an industrial nation more vulnerable to attack in time of war. In addition, with the proliferation of nuclear power plants, theft of bomb-making material becomes more feasible, and saboteurs and terrorists could begin to make their own nuclear bombs, menacing entire communities and even the nation itself.

The current debate over the construction of large numbers of nuclear power plants could be explored in greater detail. The class might investigate why insurance companies will not fully insure against damage from nuclear power plants. International ramifications may be explored by examining the wisdom of former President Nixon's offer of nuclear power plants to Israel and Egypt, India's explosion of a nuclear device, and the probable development of atomic weapons by a number of secondary powers.

The unsolved problems of nuclear wastes could also be investigated. With present technology there is no satisfactory solution to the long-range dangers of radioactive wastes. Sooner or later substantial quantities of highly radioactive wastes are likely to escape into the environment with damaging consequences no one can fully foretell. Is it wise to proceed with large scale nuclear reactor development in the hope that solutions may be found some time in the future? Are we dooming future generations, imposing on them the responsibility for containing these wastes for thousands of years?

Any modern problem, readily identified by the headlines in newspapers, has similar intricate political, social, and economic interrelationships. The energy crisis, for example, has many facets—the emerging power of oil-rich Arab nations, the economic effects of oil depletion allowances, the practices of monopolisitic and multinational companies, the negative effects of more costly energy on food production in underdeveloped nations through higher prices for fertilizer and fuel, economic changes produced by the flow of billions of dollars into a few hands in a few small nations, and the effect of higher fuel prices on mass transit, vacationing habits, and decay of cities. Once students understand this big idea of the interrelationships between elements of modern life, they will be able to generate their own examples from current news and reports from their readings in history and social studies.

PHYSICS AND THE INDUSTRIAL REVOLUTION

Superficially a traditional subject such as physics, with its studies of heat, light, mechanics, sound, electricity, and nuclear reactions, may seem to the uninitiated to have little connection with the subject of history. Every learned person knows that there is a relationship, but the average student may or may not observe this in his physics or history class. The following lesson in physics could just as well be initiated by a history teacher or by a general science teacher at a lower level.

A standard assignment in physics is calculating the cost of electricity, based on the kilowatt-hour as a unit of energy. A reality-minded physics teacher could pose a problem such as this:

A building is being constructed, and the engineer has a choice of hiring men to carry bricks to the upper floors or using an elevator operated by an electric motor. Use the following facts to compare costs for each method:
1. Electrical energy costs 5 cents per kilowatt-hour.
2. A motor using 1,000 watts of electrical energy produces one horsepower.
3. One horsepower equals ten manpower.
4. The prevailing wage for laborers carrying bricks is $3 per hour (it may be substantially higher in some regions).

The comparison is easy enough to make. The 1,000-watt motor uses one kilowatt of power an hour and costs 5 cents an hour to operate. With the standard formula, this calculation could also be stated as:

$$\text{Cost} = \frac{\text{Watts} \times \text{Hours} \times \text{Rate}}{1,000}$$

$$= \frac{1,000 \times 1 \times \$.05}{1,000}$$

$$= \$.05$$

Even if the cost of using the motor is doubled because of the original price of the equipment, depreciation, and maintenance, the cost is still only one cent an hour for the equivalent of one man's work. The cost for the work performed by an electric motor is one three-hundredths as much as a man working for $3 an hour.

In this simple calculation students can see clearly why there is so much economic pressure to replace men with machines that do hard physical work. This "big idea" is the key to understanding the Industrial Revolution and the drive to invent machines to perform men's labor. This "big idea" is also essential to comprehending the problems of developing countries that do not yet have machines and know-how to do the required physical work. Students can begin to appreciate the difficulties faced by a poor farmer in India who has no tractor to pull his plow or electric pump to draw water or help thresh grain.

The teacher can point out that a similar cost-reducing process is now taking the place of mental labor as computers perform jobs requiring calculations, memory storage, and record keeping. Students can see that such new technology produces an economic revolution that extends the Industrial Revolution into new realms. They might attempt to forecast some long-range changes that could ensue.

Labor-saving concepts may be enhanced in a physics, economics, or history class by undertaking some simple out-of-class experiments. A group of four or five students might see how long it takes them to push a car for one block with reasonable effort, then estimate how long it would take to push it one mile. They could then compute how much it would cost if they were hired to move the car, perhaps at $2 or $3 an hour. If it takes two hours for four people to push a car a mile at a labor cost of $2 an hour, the cost would be $16, but a car using gasoline costs only about 13 cents a mile to operate, and at very much greater speed. The ratio of costs for man and machine is in the neighborhood of about one hundred to one.

A similar experiment could be done with an electronic calculator. The type of calculations posed in the previous section on the annual growth of population for a period of time can be completed in a matter of minutes with an ordinary pocket calculator that provides for multiplication by a constant (K). It doesn't matter to the calculator if the growth rate is 10 percent or 3 percent or 1.45 percent. Even students who are experts at computation would have difficulty completing this task accurately in a matter of hours, or even days, especially for a growth rate such as 1.45 percent. Any error early in the series of multiplications, even if minor, causes ever-increasing inaccuracies as calculation proceeds, so human calculators must continually check their work and avoid any mistakes. Very few students can complete such a job accurately. The enormous savings achieved by the calculator in cost of mental work can be dramatically brought home by such a real experience of a contest between man and machine.

ANALYSIS OF ADVERTISING

Normally, young people tend to believe what they read or see in the media, or at least not to question it. Yet it is vital in our modern world for people to develop critical attitudes that evaluate and judge the flood of information that assaults them at every turn. Analyzing advertisements in newspapers, radio, and TV provides an excellent reality-centered way to develop such skills. Here is a typical ad for an insurance policy paraphrased from a popular magazine of the type that students often read.

A *Terrific INSURANCE Value*!!

$1,000 A MONTH
For One Day, One Month, or For Life

PAY ONLY 25¢ TO PUT THIS POLICY INTO EFFECT IMMEDIATELY.

Thereafter pay only $5.00 a month.

THIS POLICY pays you from the first day while hospitalized because of injury from ANY accident caused by an unintended external and violent force, independent of all other causes such as bodily infirmity or disease. Sprains, back strains, and hernias are not covered.

You get universal protection, anywhere, anytime you are injured.

Send This Application Today With Only 25¢

The following questions might be asked about this advertisement. Typical answers are given in brackets.

Would a person be paid if he had a heart attack, or cancer, or tuberculosis, or any bacterial or virus disease? [No. Diseases of any kind are not covered. The policy refers only to accidents.]

Would a person be paid for a hospital stay if he is hit by someone during an argument? [Probably not, because the injury is intended by the person causing the injury. Only unintended accidents are covered.]

Would he be paid for hospitalization because of exposure to heat or frost? [Perhaps not, because exposure may not be considered to involve a violent force. Other accidents that might not be covered are damage to eyes because of excessive light, injury to ears because of unusual sounds, lung damage by fumes, and the like.]

Would an elderly person be paid for hospitalization if he or she fell down the stairs? [Perhaps not, if the company could claim that the fall was caused by the fact that the person suffered from a "bodily infirmity."]

Would payment be made to a person who hurts his back while picking up a heavy object? [No. Back strains are not covered. Also this condition does not necessarily involve a violent force.]

Would the policy cover a person who is mentally disabled as a result of an accident? [Probably not because the disability is a mental problem, not a "bodily injury."]

A man breaks a leg in an accident, stays in the hospital two days, and then goes home to recuperate. He is out of work for two months. What will he be paid? [He will be paid only 2/30 of $1000 for two days in the hospital or $66.66, and nothing for the time spent at home. He must be in a hospital to receive any money. The amount paid will not be enough to cover the cost of hospital care and doctor's fees.]

A woman goes to the hospital because of an accident. After a week, she is discharged and enters a nursing home for several months. What income will she receive from the policy? [She will be paid only for the week in the hospital—about $250. A nursing home is not a hospital.]

Is this policy worth $60 a year? This question involves judgments about costs based on actual examination of specific cases. It is a relatively large sum especially for low income families. There are so many exclusions that the protection is very marginal.

Why does the ad feature the statement PAY ONLY 25¢ TO PUT THIS POLICY INTO EFFECT IMMEDIATELY? [The wording gives the impression that the policy costs only 25¢ a month.]

Why does the ad feature the phrases $1000 A MONTH and ONLY 25¢? [The size of the type and its placement are intended to mislead the reader. The exceptions that make the policy use-less in most cases of hospitalization are given in much smaller type and stated in difficult language—all purposely giving the reader the wrong impression. The ad presents false information by various language tricks, and this is done quite consciously by the person who wrote it, a fact that may shock some young people but of which they should be made aware.]

The policy says it covers ANY accident. Does it? [No, there is the modification ". . . caused by an unintended external and violent force, independent of all other causes such as bodily infirmity or disease." These gross exclusions cancel out the meaning of "ANY"—in effect, its use is equivalent to a lie.]

TV commercials provide equally interesting material for an-alysis. A breakfast cereal company displays its product with a sequence of sport scenes—bicycling, skiing, swimming, basketball—as though it is nutritionally superior to a breakfast of milk, whole wheat bread, eggs, and fruit. A bank entices customers with two famous actors chatting while a violinist plays sweet music in the background. What does that have to do with banking? An-other commercial for a bank features a famous baseball player in a series of homey scenes with ordinary people. A fruit drink com-pany displays its product against a background of waterfalls and swaying dancers. In a suntan lotion advertisement a very beautiful brown-skinned girl in a bikini walks seductively along a beach as all the males turn to watch. An inexpensive wine is promoted with a scene of a handsome young man making discreet advances to a beautiful young woman across a restaurant as though all he needed to make a conquest is a bottle of the wine, which, of course, is prominently displayed on the table. The commerical for a pill to alleviate the effects of eating too much begins with a painful after-meal scene and ends with a smiling husband who loves his wife because she gave him the pill.

What does a popular soft drink have to do with "You've got a lot to live?" What is the connection between a tiger and gasoline or a cheetah and a car? Will one have a better ride in an airplane because a beautiful hostess seductively suggests "Fly me?" Does the phrase "doctor-tested" have any significance in evaluating a product? Can one be sure that "a leading brand" of detergent selected for comparison on a test of dissolving power means that it is the best one of the competing brands available? And who decided what kind of dirt stain to remove? Does an insurance company have a better policy because one buys "a piece of the rock?"

TV and radio ads offer an almost unlimited variety of misleading devices and tricks to investigate. Analysis can extend to consumer protection, value systems, and the reasoning and objectivity of newspaper accounts and political speeches. Such studies involve the basic skill of logical thinking, which is a neglected area in the curriculum, although usually inserted as a general objective.

It is important not to push students so far that they do not believe anything they read, hear, or see in the media. Many commercials and advertisements are informative and valid, for example, a new glue that can repair a vase in a minute, a local store advertising a sale of standard luggage at a lower price, or a company showing the wide variety of its products. And, of course, most of the news in the media is "true," although one may wonder why it was selected and what was omitted. Students should be given a sense of balance in evaluating the flow of information they confront daily.

English teachers probably have more leeway in how they handle such studies than other teachers since analysis of the meaning of language is one of their goals. But a science teacher could legitimately analyze advertisements and commercials as part of a unit on methods of science and to help develop constructively skeptical attitudes. A math teacher could analyze ads by calculating costs or even as an example of logical thinking.

INVESTIGATING PREDICTIONS

Predictions about the future abound in our complex society. At one extreme are the daily astrology or horoscope columns, which purport to predict human events on the basis of date of birth and positions of the sun, moon, planets, and stars. At the other extreme was the prediction of astronomers that Pioneer 10, the first spaceship sent to photograph the planet Jupiter, would arrive, after a 21 month 100 million mile journey, at a certain point 81,000 miles from the surface of Jupiter at 7:42 A.M. eastern standard time on December 3, 1973. They were somewhat disappointed when it actually arrived there one minute late. Now *that's* a prediction!

Assessing the truth or falseness of predictions involves observing events and actually checking what occurs at appropriate times. Analyzing predictions can begin in a simple way with the weather predictions printed on some calendars or in *The Farmer's Almanac*. If one of these is available, it can be the basis of an informative class or group project. It is interesting for students to make their own predictions purely by random guessing, taking into account the local weather. June weather is usually fair most of the time, so if students predict fair weather for every day during that month, they tend to be correct as often or more often than the predictions printed on calendars or in the *Almanac*.

Students will inquire how it is possible to forecast the weather for a particular day a year in advance when daily vagaries make it difficult for meteorologists to predict weather even a day or two ahead. They might also wonder how a widely distributed calendar could possibly apply to different localities, especially if they are large distances apart.

Daily predictions by the weather services are more accurate than the long-range predictions made by students or calendars, but the difficulty of deciding what the weather really will be is complicated if it must be described in one or two words. In the morning the weather may be cloudy with a few sprinkles, then clear up by noon and remain sunny the rest of the day. Or the sky may be clear all night, followed with clouds and rain during the day. Often it is not possible to characterize a day with one word such as clear or rainy or cloudy. Students can realize why daily weather predictions often include a phrase such as "probability of rain 20 percent." They may also begin to see why long-range calendar predictions could claim to be correct if they use a simple phrase to characterize a complex, changing situation. On a day that is cloudy and windy in the morning with some rain, and sunny in the afternoon, any one-word prediction such as "cloudy," "windy," "rainy," or "sunny" could be accepted by an uncritical observer.

Economic predictions, particularly of the stock market, cost of living indices, or Gross National Product are interesting to follow up. It is essential for government, business, and labor to make predictions to guide their planning for the future, and often their predictions are more correct than not for the short run. It is educational for young people to follow through and check predictions against what really occurs. Sometimes, especially during periods of crisis or rapid change, predictions are very wrong, almost ludicrously so. For example, in January 1973 a price freeze had stabilized prices, American participation in the Vietnam War was coming to an end, and prospects for peace looked good. The general thrust of economic predictions was that the period ahead would be one of relatively stable prices, substantial economic growth, and rising stock markets. When prices were unfrozen, one of the worst inflationary spirals in American history followed, accompanied by a violent international assault on the dollar, an Arab-Israeli war, an energy crisis triggered in part by an Arab boycott, and falling stock market prices. Could anyone have predicted such a complex pattern of events?

Predictions by astrologers and other seers may be subjected to similar analysis. The standard technique of those who claim to be able to foresee the future is to make a large number of predictions, depend upon time to wipe out the memory of the full list—especially the ones that prove to be untrue—and then widely publicize the one or two that accidentally happen to come true, or seem to be true. An objective analysis is simple—just keep a record of all predictions and see what percentage actually take place.

An excellent source for such a classroom analysis is the annual listing of top astrologers' predictions published in each January issue of the *National Enquirer*, available at many newsstands. The teacher may maintain a file of past predictions and have students observe for themselves the extent of inaccuracies and the methods of exaggerating the one or two generally vague predictions that may be interpreted to have come "true."

It is instructive to have students make their own predictions. They will sometimes turn out to be as good as those made by professionals. In part, this will be accidental, but some students with more information or better judgments, or who are more clever at formulating generalized statements will tend to be more successful. The overall low rate of success will be quite comparable to that of professional astrologers and often stock market analysts as well.

The daily horoscopes printed in newspapers are a form of prediction that may also be subjected to objective analysis. When students check horoscopes and relate them to reality, they soon discover for themselves how slippery the statements are because of their vague generalities, "Today is a good day to be cautious of financial entanglements." If one is cautious and no financial loss ensues, was the prediction correct? How cautious is cautious? If one buys a camera, is that a financial entanglement? Is it a financial entanglement for a rich man as well as a poor man? If one spends money for a camera and then loses or accidentally drops it, was the prediction true? Suppose there is a defect in the camera that can be fixed in one trip to the store—does this verify the astrologer's warning?

This kind of analysis reveals to students how astrologers thrive on vague general advice that could be applicable to everyone. They also learn that many facts are difficult to verify or interpret— a "big idea" that could help them make more intelligent judgments later in life.

The personality profile based on birth date offered by astrologers is a form of prediction that is difficult to analyze because of the complexity of the human personality. The subjective criteria used to evaluate aspects of personality are excellent subjects for study, providing rich concept development for students. A good way to begin an investigation is for the students to list personality characteristics of friends or relatives or of themselves, and then check these descriptions against astrologers' profiles. Students will find it difficult to describe people in simple, general terms such as aggressive, shy, or lonely, terms that may apply in some situations but not in others. Students will find it difficult to match their descriptions to those of astrologers. However, they will find it much easier the other way around because they can always find in any horoscope some characteristics of any individual; they will tend to ignore those that do not apply.

Throughout such investigations teachers should avoid making prejudgments because students often react adversely to authoritative statements and begin to look for instances where the teacher is wrong. As students attempt to find the truth for themselves, the difficulties they encounter in relating vague predictive statements to reality will convince most that they are dealing with subjective generalities. Usually there are some students who have a deep need to believe in astrology and will not be dissuaded by any argument.

At a suitable point it is important to raise questions about the theory behind a purported predictive art. Consider the claims of astrologers, for example. How could the positions of the stars affect events and personalities of all individuals born on the same day in different countries in different years? How could Jupiter's position in the sky affect financial transactions or love affairs all over the globe? Students will be unable to find any rational explanations of such cause-and-effect relationships in astrology books. At best, explanations offered are based on ancient traditions and vague beliefs that some unknown mechanisms are at work.

As an illustration of the type of causality found in astrology books, one source implies that people born under the sign of Taurus, the bull, are aggressive because bulls are aggressive. Another source indicates that people born under the sign of Aries, the ram, are supposed to have bushy eyebrows because the sign of the ram resembles bushy eyebrows. This kind of investigation will appeal to more scientific students, but the findings will be of interest to all.

History-minded students will find it fascinating to trace the cultural roots of soothsaying and astrology. The first predictable events known to man were the recurrence of the day and the seasons and the annual motions of the stars, and this led ancient man to look for other predictable events in the motions of stars and planets. Even Kepler and Newton evidenced a strange mixture of science and superstition, believing as they did in the efficacy of astrological methods. So be patient with any students (and teachers) who may be believers.

OPEN-MINDEDNESS AND HEALTHY SKEPTICISM

The teaching techniques suggested for handling predictions and astrology in the classroom may be applied to a number of similar popular fads with suitable variations. For example, there is a substantial number of UFO (Unidentified Flying Object) enthusiasts who have their own periodicals, conferences, and campaigns to obtain adherents. Recurring UFO reports are in a somewhat different category from astrology because basic beliefs are not so much the fundamental issue, although they are a factor. Instead the main questions revolve around what was observed (if it was observed) and what inferences are drawn from the observations.

Several "big ideas" may be involved in the study of UFOs. First, and most important, one must be open-minded about the possible validity of what may seem to be outlandish ideas. Various examples come to mind of ideas and speculations that seemed bizarre or even insane in the past but which are accepted today. Among these are: continents that slowly drift on the surface of the earth and collide to produce mountains or separate to form oceans, stars and galaxies billions of light years away, man evolving from hominoids and apes, the right of common people to elect their leaders, the right of women to vote, the right of a male to remove his shirt on the beach, and the right to dissent from accepted views. Other ideas and proposals now struggling for acceptance are the right of abortion, the right to walk naked on a beach, the right of quick and easy divorce, the right to live in communes, multiple marriage, complete civil rights for homosexuals, and the right of non-smokers to breathe clean air versus the right of smokers to enjoy a smoke.

Along with open-mindedness towards UFO reports, one must have a healthy skepticism toward inferences or conclusions derived from purported observations. Students need to understand that hoaxes and fakery are generally to be expected in any new and puzzling phenomenon. From reports by reasonably reliable observers it seems that something strange is seen but they don't know what it is. When reports about UFOs or flying saucers appear in the newspapers, one is struck by the differences and vagueness of what people say they saw. It is instructive for students to read ancient reports of comets described in encyclopedias and reference books in which awestruck observers, some with substantial reputations, "observed" comets to be hideous apparitions with flowing beards, flaming swords, fiery robes, or goblins.

The teacher should also discuss the likelihood of hoaxes for some of the more startling reports of UFOs, especially where real creatures and space ships are described in detail. Among the most notorious examples of a hoax was the invention of the Piltdown man by a frustrated naturalist who buried parts of an ape in his area in England and then dug them up in front of witnesses. Scientists were confused for decades by the anomalies of this find until chemical tests recently revealed the fakery. Meanwhile the "facts" had appeared in all the textbooks. A lower level of tomfoolery was the incident of a faker in New Jersey who periodically stomped around in large web-footed shoes on the shores near his home to initiate news reports of a giant bird wandering about in the area.

Some of the UFO books contain obvious hoaxes that are subject to analysis and proof by students. In one book a purported photograph of a flying saucer, supposedly snapped outdoors in daylight, is most likely a fake because of two reflection spots in the curved undersurface. The sun could never have made two reflection spots in a uniformly curved surface—a matter subject to student investigation. The picture was probably taken indoors with two floodlights. In fact, the flying saucer looks as though it were probably made from a curved hubcap or lamp fixture with three Ping-Pong balls glued to the underside. In the same book a detailed report by a neighbor who verified the passage of a flying saucer over the author's house was proven to be a fake when the neighbor subsequently sued the author for failing to pay the $500 he promised for the false story.

Another basic "good idea" that evolves from analyzing UFO reports is the tendency to make wild guesses and assumptions from observations. If a group of observers report a mysterious glowing object moving in the sky, this becomes proof to some that intelligent beings from outer space are watching our planet. No hard evidence exists, although there is established evidence for such rare phenomena as luminous ball lightning that looks like a luminous sphere and erratically moves about in a local area for a substantial period of time. Around the turn of the century a group of astronomers observing auroral effects noted an enormous cigar-shaped luminous area moving across the sky like a giant airship. With spectroscopes, they were able to see spectral lines characteristic of an auroral discharge. In other words, it is likely that some reports of flying saucers are based on an actual rare natural event, the nature of which is still not known. The intelligent citizen must reserve final judgment until evidence is definitive. The possibility that UFOs are space ships from distant civilizations cannot yet be ruled out.

Extrasensory perception or ESP is another subject of a similar category of interest to students. Very little is known about the subconscious ways in which people communicate, although past experience makes one suspicious of stories of instant communication over thousands of miles. By sheer chance very unusual events are certain to occur for some of the three billion persons on earth at some time in their lives, and when they do, they seem to be caused by a supernatural force of some kind.

Nevertheless, investigations of such phenomena by reputable authorities using improved experimental procedures has promoted new scientific and public interest and acceptance of parapsychology as an area of scientific concern.[1] To date the mixed results of the experiments are hardly conclusive. Teachers can encourage open-mindedness by discussing current articles on the subject, provided that they attempt to evaluate the trustworthiness of the source of information. Some periodicals will feature anything that is sensational to increase readership, while others attempt to be relatively objective.

As with astrology, a basic problem in handling such topics in schools is the dearth and sometimes total lack of objective books and pamphlets written at the students' level.

WEIGHING EARTH'S ATMOSPHERE

It is essential for people today to develop concepts about earth as a finite space ship carrying dependent mankind on its surface on a never-ending journey around the sun. All students should come to feel that they are but one of many riders on that globe and that, as human beings blessed with the power of thought, they have responsibility to contribute to the balance and harmony of nature. Such concepts cannot be developed in a single lesson by an inspired teacher but are best generated by many experiences and

---

[1] News item, *"Bulletin"* of the *American Association for the Advancement of Science*, vol. 19, June 1974, p. 16.

activities in many classes over a period of time. Young people should develop the feeling that the gift of thought gives them the power to perform important acts and to affect events—that they are not merely pawns of inexorable and overwhelming forces of nature.

This "big idea" may be developed by considering the question, "What is the weight of all the air in the atmosphere?" In an eighth- or ninth-grade science class the question can be raised in a natural way during a unit about air pressure, after students have studied the barometer. In a math class the question might be brought up in connection with a study of functions of the formula $y = ax^2$, or during a lesson about the area of a circle or sphere,[2] or as an application of the shorthand method of writing large numbers using exponents of 10. The matter could also be raised in any unit concerned with the environment in an English or social studies class.

At first students may think it impossible for them to perform the feat of weighing all the air on earth without complex instruments and calculating powers far beyond their ability. The idea of accomplishing the task at their desks, with only paper and pencil and in a few minutes, will seem absurd. But teachers can assure them that it can be done offering a couple of hints: 1) Air pressure at sea level is equal to about 15 pounds per square inch; and 2) The formula for the area (A) of a sphere of radius (r) is: $A = 4\pi r^2$.

It is best if the students are allowed time to work out these clues for themselves, perhaps as a homework assignment. Some creative students are likely to find solutions themselves and then show the class how to proceed. The pressure of 15 pounds per square inch is caused by the weight of a column of air, one square inch in area and extending all the way up to the outer limits of the atmosphere. The total weight of all the air (in pounds) in the at-

---

[2] $A = 4\pi r^2$ belongs to the class of equations of the form $y = ax^2$.

mosphere, therefore, is equal to 15 pounds times the number of square inches on the earth's surface at sea level. Thus:

15 lbs/sq. in. × area of earth's surface (sq. in.)
$W = 15 \times 4\pi r^2$ lbs. (where r is in *inches*)

The radius of the earth is approximately 4,000 miles, a distance that can be changed to inches by multiplying by 5,280 and then by 12. Therefore:

$W = 15 \times 4\pi \times (4{,}000 \times 5{,}280 \times 12)^2$ lbs.
$W = 15 \times 4 \times 3.14 \times 4{,}000 \times 4{,}000 \times 5{,}280 \times 5{,}280 \times 12 \times 12$ lbs.
$W = 12{,}000{,}000{,}000{,}000{,}000{,}000$ lbs. (approx.)
$W = 12 \times 10^{18}$ lbs. (approx.)
$W = 12$ thousand million billion lbs.

Some creative students may challenge certain assumptions in this calculation, and they should be encouraged to do so. For example, these calculations assume that the entire surface of the earth is at sea level, which is obviously not so because of hills and mountains. Since most hills do not rise above sea level more than a few thousand feet and mountains rarely rise above a mile, whereas the atmosphere extends upward for over a hundred miles, any correction for this factor is, at best, a relatively small one. Some students may wish to pursue these corrections as a special project.

Another source of error may seem to arise from the fact that the one-square-inch columns, assumed in the calculation, taper outward slightly as they radiate outward from the center of the earth. At the upper levels of the atmosphere one would expect the one square inch area to be enlarged slightly. Actually, this factor does not alter the calculation because gravitational force also radiates outward along these same columns and is reduced at high altitudes in the same proportion as the area is increased. Consideration of this point could lead to a very interesting project for advanced students.

A calculation of this kind can be a startling, exciting, and deeply satisfying experience—the knowledge that one can perform the Herculean feat of weighing all the air on earth merely by taking one measurement with a barometer and assuming that the earth's radius is 4,000 miles. Creative students may obtain the confidence to tackle similar big investigations: How much oxygen does all the plant life on earth release every year? How much carbon dioxide do plants use up? How much carbon dioxide is released into the atmosphere by man's burning of fossil fuel? How does this upset the balances of nature? How much sunlight reaches the earth from the sun? What are the limits to production of food from sunlight?

It will be necessary for students to use library resources and perhaps consult local specialists at universities, but appropriate information can be handled by some high school students. Once basic information is obtained and included in reports, it may be retained in the school library for use by future students.

EPILOGUE

The ever-increasing complexity of life today constantly generates new situations and problems that involve every child and adult. No one can escape the necessity of facing these problems on an individual or group basis. Young people must be taught techniques of solving the individual and group problems created by change. Failure to develop successful ways of solving problems can only promote feelings of frustration, despair, withdrawal, and alienation—disturbing frames of mind that are increasing today.

The structure, content, and methodology of schooling developed in the past for a slower changing environment can no longer serve as a model for today's society. A critical shift of emphasis and approach is needed in which what students learn—and how they learn it—constantly involves problem-solving in a realistic setting with a maximum of applicability.

Reality-centered learning can produce many pluses in terms of individual learning. Motivation is stronger when students feel a subject is meaningful to them, as is the case when content deals with real things and real problems. All the desired objectives of education—accumulation of knowledge, development of basic skills and abilities, clarification of appropriate values, and the ability to make intelligent decisions and judgments—are more likely to be realized in a framework of reality-centered learning-by-doing.

Schools must now be transformed into learning environments that are integrally meshed with the world in which students must learn to live.

In the foregoing chapters, the authors have offered numerous examples of reality-centered learning approaches for the secondary level in the hope that teachers and administrators will adapt these to their own educational situations.

But that is the least of it. "Talk is cheap" and so are words. What ultimately counts is the transformation of words into meaningful action. The learning-by-doing principle is as applicable to teachers as to students. No book can effect change without active doing-participation of the intended audience. The only way teachers, and school systems as well, can begin to develop reality-centered approaches and techniques is to get their hands dirty and their feet wet with actual attempts to utilize the kinds of suggestions described in this book. In the course of wrestling with the real-life problems of a reality-centered program, educators will inevitably create and develop new ways of giving life to school learning. In so doing, they will be helping their students to live fuller, richer, and more meaningful lives in a difficult yet potentially fruitful period of human history.

BIBLIOGRAPHY

AIKEN, W. M., ed. *Story of the Eight Year Study*. New York: Harper & Row, 1942.

AMIDON, E. J., and FLANDERS, N. A. *The Role of the Teacher in the Classroom*, rev. ed. Association for Productive Teaching, 1040 Plymouth Building, Minneapolis, Minn. 55402, 1967.

ANDERSON, G. *The Assessment of Learning Environments*. Halifax Nova Scotia: Atlantic Institute of Education, 1971.

Association for Supervision and Curriculum Development (ASCD). *To Nurture Humaneness: Commitment for the 70s*. Washington, D. C.: ASCD, 1970.

AUSUBEL, D. P. *The Psychology of Meaningful Verbal Learning*. New York: Grune and Stratton, 1963.

BELLACK, A. A. et. al. *The Language of the Classroom*. New York: Columbia University Press, 1966.

Biological Sciences Curriculum Study (BSCS). *Human Sciences: A Developmental Approach to Adolescent Education*. Boulder, Colo.: Biological Sciences Curriculum Study Committee, 1973.

BLOOM, B., and KRATHWOHL, P. R., eds. *Taxonomy of Educational Objectives: Cognitive and Affective Domains.* New York: David McKay, 1956.

CARR, W. G., ed. *Values and the Curriculum: A Report of the Fourth International Curriculum Conference.* Washington, D.C.: National Education Association, Center for Study of Instruction, 1970.

COLEMAN, J. S. et al. *Youth: Transition to Adulthood, Report of Panel on Youth, President's Science Advisory Committee.* Chicago: University of Chicago Press, 1974.

COOPER, E. L. "Social Changes, Popular Music and the Teacher," *Social Education,* December 1973.

CRARY, R. *Humanizing the School: Curriculum Development and Theory.* New York: Knopf, 1969.

DAVIES, R. A., ed. *School Library Media Center: A Force for Educational Excellence,* 2nd ed. New York: R. R. Bowker, 1974.

DOLL, R. C. "Alternative Forms of Schooling," *Educational Leadership,* February 1972.

ERIKSON, E. *Childhood and Society.* New York: W. W. Norton, 1950.

FEATHERSTONE, J. *Schools Where Children Learn.* New York: Liveright, 1971.

Film Utilization Catalogue, special ed. Learning Corporation of America, 711 Fifth Ave., New York, N.Y. 10022, 1974.

The Fleischmann Report on the Quality, Cost, and Financing of Elementary and Secondary Education in New York State, 3 vols. New York: Viking Press, 1973.

FREDERICK, W. C., and KLAUSMEIER, H. J. "Cognitive Styles: A Description," *Educational Leadership,* April 1970.

GARTNER, ALAN et al. *Children Teach Children: Learning by Teaching.* New York: Harper & Row, 1971.

GATTEGNO, C. *Toward a Visual Culture: Educating Through Television.* New York: Outerbridge, 1969.

GETZELS, J. W., and JACKSON, P. W. *Creativity and Intelligence: Explorations with Gifted Students.* New York: John Wiley, 1962.

GLINES, D. E. *Creating Humane Schools.* Mankato, Minn.: Campus Publishers, 1971.

GORMAN, RICHARD M. *Discovering Piaget: A Guide for Teachers.* Columbus: Charles E. Merrill, 1972.

GRAMBS, J. D. et al. *Modern Methods in Secondary Education,* 3rd ed. New York: Holt, Rinehart and Winston, 1970.

GREENBERG, J. D., and ROUSH, R. E. "A Visit to a School Without Walls: Two Impressions." *Phi Delta Kappan,* May 1970.

GROSS, B., and GROSS, R., eds. *Radical School Reform*. New York: Simon and Shuster, 1970.

GUILFORD, J. P. *The Nature of Human Intelligence*. New York: Mc-Graw-Hill, 1967.

————. "Roles of the Structure-of-Intellect Abilities in Education," *Journal of Research and Development in Education*, Spring, 1971.

HOFFMAN, B. *The Tyranny of Testing*. New York: Crowell Collier, 1962.

HOLT, J. *Why Children Fail*. New York: Dell Publishing Co., 1964.

JAHODA, M. *Race Relations and Mental Health*. Paris, France: UNESCO, 1960.

KENWORTHY, LEONARD. *Background Papers for Social Studies Teachers*. Belmont, Calif.: Wadsworth Publishing Co., 1966.

KUNEN, J. S. "The Rebels of the 70s," *New York Times Magazine*, October 28, 1973.

MASLOW, A. H. *Motivation and Personality*. New York: Harper & Row, 1954.

Nuffield Foundation. Science Teaching Project. Chelsea College, Unitversity of London; New York: Penguin Books, Inc., 1970.

RANCE, P. *Teaching by Topics*. London: Ward Lock, 1968.

RATHS, L. E. *Meeting the Needs of Children: Creating Trust and Security*. Columbus, Ohio: Charles E. Merrill, 1970.

———— et al. *Values and Teaching: Working with Values in the Classroom*. Columbus, Ohio: Charles E. Merrill, 1966.

REISCHAUER, E. O. *Toward the 21st Century: Education for a Changing World*. New York: Knopf, 1973.

RICHMOND, G. *The Micro-Society School*. New York: Harper & Row, 1973.

ROGERS, C. R. *Freedom to Learn: A View of What Education Might Become*. Columbus, Ohio: Charles E. Merrill, 1969.

ROLLINS, J. et al. "Developing Multiple Talents in Classrooms Through the Implementation of Research," *Journal of Research and Development in Education*, Spring, 1971.

ROMEY, W. D. *Risk, Trust, Love: Learning in a Humane Environment*. Columbus, Ohio: Charles E. Merrill, 1972.

RUCHLIS, H. *Guidelines to Education of Nonreaders*. Brooklyn, N.Y.: Book-Lab, Inc., 1972.

SCHMUCK, P., and SCHMUCK, R. *Group Processes in the Classroom*. Dubuque, Iowa: William C. Brown, 1970.

SILBERMAN, C. E. *Crisis in the Classroom: The Remaking of American Education*. New York: Random House, 1970; Vintage, pap.